BEYOND THE EMERGING CHURCH

THE END AND THE BEGINNING OF A MOVEMENT

By

Thomas Hohstadt

Damah Media
3522 Maple Avenue
Odessa, Texas 79762

ISBN 0-9672944-2-8

Online Orders:
www.FutureChurch.net

Cover photo by Mark Thiessen

To

My Family

Muriel
Lowell, Kathy, Sarah Joy, & Jonathan
Dan, Leslie, Danny, & Mya Marie

All in ministry
All with a vision for the Church

TABLE OF CONTENTS

INTRODUCTION

The "Tipping Point"

Something real and reliable matters! For when the ship starts sinking, everyone reaches for the life preservers.

Leading thinkers agree we live in a time of explosive change, epic metamorphosis, perhaps the most precipitous moment in planetary history.[1] During this century alone, we'll see—at today's rate—on the order of 20,000 years of change.[2] And, the next viable human community will differ decidedly from what we've called "civilization."[3]

Warnings like these can't be brushed aside! The very future of faith depends on emerging church leaders "getting it." And they have only a few years—25 is a conservative guess—to get it right.[4]

If they fail, we all fail.

Alarmingly, we've already reached the "tipping point" between the failure and the success of the "emerging church movement." We've already moved into lands where even our best maps no longer work. And, we've already faced inescapable history and risked unredeemable errors.

Trapped in "Glass Houses"

It wasn't always that way.

The early emerging church movement responded to the signs of the times: the sober warnings of a *post-Christendom* reality. In the beginning, its diverse and innovative leaders were neither "rebels" nor "heretics." They were, instead, a fragile and fluid, transparent and pristine "emergence" *within* the church. They envisioned a more "relevant" God, a more "real" God, a more "personal" God *within* the "official" God. They focused on alternative worship for younger generations—but with the goal of making these generations part of the church again. . . .

. . . they had hoped!

Tragically, many emerging leaders got burned by the pseudo-sacred realities of today's church. They discovered a church either totally out of touch with the world or totally in touch with the world—a world the Lord of History had already left behind. They found long-established leaders in positions of power holding stubbornly to where God had been at the expense of where God was going. And they found hidden hierarchies ignoring a future world in order to pacify a past sanity.

This proved too much frustration for those who were already frustrated. It required too much care for those who already cared. So, in the middle of the night, the movement crossed a forbidden boundary, and—perhaps unintentionally—became a source of controversy, a target of criticism.

With many critics, the "emerging church" implied trauma and chaos. The movement seemed far-out and foreign, counter-cultural and conspiratorial. And, by most doctrines, it sounded even "dangerous." One well-known group, for example, has been called "off base at best and heretical at worst."[5]

Incredibly, though, many emerging church leaders have become their worst enemy. They have polarized differences with the church and proclaimed *entirely unnecessary* offences. Indeed, when traditional Christendom leaders finally hear what's being said, they'll call it "scandalous."

The movement is also embarrassingly self-contradictory, doing the very things it despises, embracing the very things it rejects, and making the very mistakes it pins on others.

How can the nascent leaders of the future be so naive? Those leaders who yearn most for renewal actually obstruct it! They have unwittingly created labels that the world now uses to silence them.

They have trapped themselves in "glass houses."

An Apology and a Wake-Up Call

It's worrying when a movement this young becomes the target of criticism.

Will the "emerging church" really emerge? Or, will it become an infamous oxymoron—"submerging" rather than "emerging"? We wonder, after all, if it will become a mere blip on the radar of time?—a stylish fad for the disaffected few?—a rapture for nerds?—a grace for geeks? . . . And, we wonder if we're just repeating past mistakes?

Is the movement *"deja vu* all over again"?

I'm a member of the emerging church. In fact, I was a member of renewal movements several years before the term "emerging church" was invented. In other words, I've had plenty of time to make plenty of mistakes. This book is an apology for those mistakes and a wake-up call for my friends in the emerging church movement.

Obviously, it's too early to nail down final definitions for this movement, but I know what I know and I write what I see. The leaders of the movement may deny what I see, but what they do—or rather, what they *say* they do—hides an embarrassing whitewash of wishful thinking.

We still need an emerging church movement. We still need a prophetic vision for the church. So let us fervently believe this movement is *yet to emerge*. Let us humbly concede we're capable of confessing our hidden biases. And, let us profoundly yearn for the miracles of *His* hope rather than the manipulations of *our* hope.

What, then, are these "hidden biases"?

Endnotes

1. Thomas Berry, Mitchell Stevens, Ray Kurzweil, Steven Johnson, Henry Kissinger, Alvin Toffler, and many others.

2. Ray Kurzweil in PC Magazine, September 4, 2001, p. 151, 153.

3. Thomas Berry, quoted in Gene Marshall, *Fresh Wineskins for the Christian Breakthrough: Fragments of Visionary Brooding on the Sociological Future of Christianity*, (Realistic Living Press, Bonham, TX, 1999) p. 50.

4. The approximate watershed moment predicted by futurists of "Technological Singularity." See: http://en.wikipedia.org/wiki/ Technological_singularity

5. Peter Walker and Tyler Clark, "Missing the Point?" *Relevant Magazine*, Issue 21, July-August, 2006, pp 70-74.

PART ONE

HIDDEN BIASES

A PHILOSOPHICAL FAD

The "Holy Grail" of Postmodernism

Most would-be futurists cling to the "Holy Grail" of postmodernism. They blindly adhere to every novelty of this philosophical fad. In fact, *the very definition* of the "emerging church" includes this philosophy—or, what many now consider, this *failed* philosophy.

No doubt, something needs to challenge the harmful excess of modern thinking. Something needs to question the manipulating self-interests of our small worlds. Something needs to expose the distortion of our rhetoric, the slant on our slang, the leanings of our lingo. And, something needs to refuse the arrogance of our "God in a box."

But, with too many gullible postmodernists, "One enormously precious baby was tossed with tons of unpleasant bathwater."[1]

Postmodernism, after all, angrily rejects the modern past. It arrogantly "deconstructs" a "truthful" present—especially everybody else's truth!—and it cynically proposes a hopeless future. In short, Truth—with a capital "T"—no longer exists: "Absolute truth is an illusion and one interpretation is purportedly as good as any other."[2]

Yet, the claims of postmodernists get a little embarrassing. Their "authoritative announcements" that "there is no authority" get a little befuddled. After all, "To say there are no absolutes is in itself absolute."[3]

But postmodernists ignore these inconsistencies. "Truth is whatever you want it to be, it's whatever suits your purpose." In other words, "You do your thing, and I'll do mine." Their "new world," then, becomes an anarchy of endless private opinions—a sea of disconnected dots. So a "move of the Spirit" easily becomes lawless license. An "anointing" often becomes knee-jerk reflex. And a "manifestation of God" usually becomes one more psychological condition.

Still more embarrassing, "postmodernism" has **already come and gone**. This fad is about the death of the past, and the past has already past! "Postmodernism is so yesterday . . . To deconstruct everybody else's ideas . . . just (isn't) any fun anymore."[4]

Obviously, we live in a "post-modern" period, but we must not confuse it with "postmodern*ism*." Something else has already replaced this fleeting philosophy.

There are profound implications, for example, beyond mere subjectivity. There are vast worlds of prophetic visions, inspired revelations, and vicarious beauties far more significant than mere opinions, self-made notions, or selfish beliefs. There is even a language beyond language that transcends us, language itself, and the culture in which it "speaks."

Truth, after all, is autonomous. It's not something we create—it's something we encounter. It's a "not us." It has an "is-ness" or existence prior to our interpretation. And, it has self-evident signs and self-authenticating tests that differ, for the most part, from the "proofs" we've misused for so many years.

In short, wiping the slate clean removes neither God nor His Truth.

Endnotes

1. Ken Wilber, *A Theory of Everything: An Integral Vision for Business, Politics, Science, and Spirituality* (Boston: Shambhala, 2000) p. 81, 82.

2. Lewis Edwin Hahn, Editor, *The Philosophy of Paul Ricoeur* (Chicago: Open Court, 1995) pp. 278-280.

3. Leonard Sweet, quoted in Peter Walker and Tyler Clark, "Missing the Point?" *Relevant Magazine*, Issue 21, July-August, 2006, pp 70-74.

4. Wilber, p. ix, x.

Which World Do You Live In?

It's important to know where we live! Do you live in the world of "modernism," "postmodernism," or somewhere else? How do you know?

Take the following test to confirm where you stand. Select which statement in each group best describes your opinion. Then, at the end of the following five groups, we will discover the world you live in and whether you are working with or against the Lord of History.

––––––––––––––––– ••◗◉◖•• –––––––––––––––––

A. The Church will be ready for the future if it retains its vision of progress—if it continually improves what it is already doing.

B. The modern idea of progress is an illusion. The Church can no longer move into the future by simply improving itself.

C. Instead of focusing on the death of old thinking, we need to focus on the birth of a newly empowered and profoundly faithful way of thinking.

––––––––––––––––– ••◗◉◖•• –––––––––––––––––

A. Scripture is a storehouse of facts that accurately describes reality, so our challenge is to faithfully figure out the facts.

B. Scripture does not contain facts. It is a relative truth, because its writers and readers never escaped their subjectivity or the inadequacy of their language.

C. Scripture speaks only through the voice of the Spirit and transcends both interpreters and interpretations. We must learn, therefore, to let Scripture speak for itself.

A. The most persuasive sermons build logical lines of thought which arrive at sound theological doctrines.

B. "Logical lines of thought" have never proven what the modern world promised. It's time to wipe the slate clean.

C. "Wiping the slate clean" removes neither God nor His Truth. "Truth" is not something we subjectively invent. It is a reality we encounter.

A. Skilled rhetoric and great oratory prove the best hope for spreading the "Word."

B. All languages reflect our manipulating self-interest and our blind subjectivity. So we will never bring objective honesty to the Word or anything else.

C. The Church has known a spiritual language that transcends our opinions, our language, our doctrines, and the cultures that have invented them. This language is the only language of the Word.

A. An authentic interpretation of the Gospel requires setting aside our emotions and feelings.

B. All interpretations of the Gospel are subjective, so the only "realities" are one's own opinions and feelings. That's the reason we should avoid telling others what to believe.

C. The Church has long known a "knowing of the heart" that transcends our subjectivity—our intellect—and our differences. This "knowing" is essential to the future of the Gospel.

If you selected mostly "A" statements, you are firmly stuck in the modern period. If you selected mostly "B" statements, consider yourself a postmodernist. However, if you selected mostly "C" statements, you are probably following the Lord of History.

These conclusions are simplistic, of course, but their combined force pry open many unexplored doors within the emerging church movement.

AN ARMCHAIR CHRISTIANITY

The "Very Heart" of Christianity?

Many emerging leaders remain indifferent to *doing* the church. They prefer, instead, *thinking* the church. They focus, for example, on dialogue and discussion. Their core convictions manifest armchair "Christianity." So they ceaselessly talk and blog, "deconstruct" and "reconstruct."

As a result, church mission reduces to abstract "mission"—more a mind set than a model—more the nature than the need—more process than practice. In other words, their "mission" morphs more toward "knowing" than "doing" or "being." In fact, "philosophical discussion"—according to a well-known leader—is at the "very heart" of Christianity.

That would surprise Jesus.

Of course, the problems are obvious: inaction in place of action—contemplation in place of improvisation—teaching in place of modeling—labeling in place of experiencing. Such imbalances lead to passive lethargy, pathological sleepiness, alarming unresponsiveness. . . .

. . . and impotent, Milquetoast believers.

Pure logic, after all, never converted anyone! Rational knowledge was never the main "power." The literal world was never the main "reality." And, the lecture hall was never the main "Word." Paul claimed, for example, "The kingdom of God consists of and is based on *not talk* but power."[1] And, today's "theology of the Spirit" doesn't come even close to Paul's "*demonstration* of the Spirit."[2]

So we end up losing something far more precious—a proactive faith, a can-do faith, an incarnate faith. In other words, "Overemphasis on *how* to do church . . . has taken the focus off Christ Himself."[3]

The future belongs to those who understand the present return to an oral culture—a place where "words" demand action, where prophetic visions co-create, and where an inspired "doing" endows *everything*.

It's not too late to finally understand that we are "coauthors" in a world not so much a Creation as a "Creating." In short, we "kick-start" every moment—in real-time and in real-life—no matter how big or how small that moment may be.

We have to. Compassion urgently unloads itself—it desperately releases itself—it begs sharing itself.[4]   Otherwise, the pain is unbearable.

> "Life is neither the candle nor the wick, but the burning."[5]

Endnotes

1. I Corinthians 4:20 *The Amplified Bible*.

2. I Corinthians 2:4, *The Amplified Bible*.

3. Leonard Sweet, quoted in Peter Walker and Tyler Clark, "Missing the Point?" *Relevant Magazine*, Issue 21, July-August, 2006, pp 70-74.

4. II Corinthians 8:4, *The Amplified Bible*.

5. Mike Riddell, Mark Pierson, Cathy Kirkpatrick, *The Prodigal Project: Journey Into the Emerging Church* (London: Society for Promoting Christian Knowledge, 2000) p. 76.

The End of Milquetoast Christianity

So a terrible virus has spread through today's church—the cold sickness of a faith that simply "thinks"—a "thinking-man's" religion. Mere words, hard facts, and the trivial surface of language hardly suffice in a world of deeper realities. So it's no surprise that today's "spiritual leaders" seldom claim "spiritual awareness." They fly blind in the Spirit, yet still expect changes in the "flesh." Indeed,

> The spiritual and social implications of Pentecost, which define the relationship of the human spirit to the Holy Spirit, *have yet to be explored* for the age in which we live.[1]

So today's faith is more passive than empowered, more anemic than energized. It's more an inert mass of doctrines—a group of dormant ideas—a collection of lethargic labels than anything else. As a result, its Milquetoast believers pretend beliefs they don't even have.

Incredible, as well, the church of a Creative God has no "theology of creativity."[2] This fact proves further today's spiritual fatigue. And this sign shows certainly that we have lost hold of the bold, inspired, and proactive faith of our spiritual fathers.

No wonder churches die day by day at the hands of the unempowered.

> "Blessed is he that expects nothing,
> for he shall never be disappointed."[3]

"Going Forth" & "Doing Things"

Yet, the trend of history offers just the opposite. It promises a new faith—an empowered faith, a prophetic faith, a deeply personal faith.

For we are returning to the *faith* of an oral culture—or more to the point, the faith of an *electronic* oral culture. Already, two-thirds of the world's population live and move in an oral culture.[4] This includes not only the stories, songs, and comic books of illiterate societies, but the Internet, TV, movies, cell phones, and computer games of *literate* societies.

So why is this important? Why should this make any difference to the emerging church?

Unlike modern "words" which merely "supervene" in life (that is, they merely "add to" life), the "words" of an oral culture "intervene" in life (they actually *change* life.) Unlike written words which passively contemplate, the empowered words of an oral community *actively co-create*. And, unlike our "educated" lingo which simply "thinks," the intrusive words of in-your-face fellowships *do things*.

This is not new truth, it's forgotten truth. This is not new wisdom, it's neglected wisdom. The Hebrews of the Bible lived in an oral culture and practiced its oral power. God spoke to them through *damah*—or "prophetic metaphor."[5] Then, their God-grounded, God-consigned, and God-impassioned metaphors went forth and *did things*.

Their believing, speaking, and creating were all the same. All three were cut from the same piece of cloth!

As a result, they possessed a profound understanding of creativity—a potent mixture of power and passion. Contrary to modern opinion, creativity pervades the entire Bible. Its language does not describe *what is*, it describes what is *coming to be*. Its foreseen future of faith and its imagined vision of creativity are the *same spiritual force*.

In other words, God created us to create!

Today, our words are more important than we ever imagined. The *casual* "word" is finished. In fact, it probably never existed.

Collaborators—Co-laborers—Co-authors

In oral worlds—both then and now—faith and creativity are one. Faith anticipates the "yet-to-be." It looks "to things that are unseen" and "perceives" the things for which we hope.[6] The poet Wordsworth echoed the same vision: A creative person is simply one affected more than others "by absent things as if they were present."[7]

More important, faith and creativity move in *simultaneous* worlds: In the moment of inspiration, faith gives form to its inspiration. In the moment of vision, faith gives "substance" to its vision.[8] Then, as we share this vision with others, we become "prophets"—because that's what prophets do!

In other words, we have a role to play. We are more partnered with the Almighty than we ever imagined. The fact that oral words "do" things means we "do" things too. Indeed, the future is more formed than found. Our passion is more applied than perceived.

After all, in an oral culture things must get expressed, feelings must be given form, the anointing must get announced. Yes, we contemplate the mystery, but we also express the mystery. Yes, we stand awed in its depth, but we also give form to that depth.

We are collaborators—co-laborers—co-authors. . . .

When whole "systems" and their parts—including us!—mutually determine one another, the role of divine action takes on an entirely new dimension:

Pregnant With the Future

The act of faith is always an *act* of faith. There's nothing passive or secondhand about it. The dynamics of faith require an intentional

"acting out." We are full-time creators in the kingdom of *"As If."*
And, giving birth to this kingdom, we are no more spectators than
Jesus was a spectator.

This is not an illusion, it's reality! Scripture insists our vision of the
future is more real than the world in which we now live, *which is
already passing away!*[9] In other words, the "actual" universe is the
one coming into being. So our present faith is pregnant with the
future, with the *not-yet* inside the *already*.

We may understand life backwards, but we live it *forwards*.

Indeed, everything we "expect" we are bringing into being. No
matter how small, no matter how insignificant, every movement,
every moment, has a never-ending ripple effect—engaging and
shaping history.

. . . for better or worse! Whether we are conscious or unconscious,
good or bad, believers or unbelievers, concerned or unconcerned,
encouraged or discouraged—one way or another, we *will* change
history.

The only question is *which way*.

So we must intentionally focus the field of our intention. We must
decide our destiny from the One who has already destined. We must
bring to pass what the Spirit has already brought to pass. This means
we "create," we don't "invent." For creative inspiration is something
spoken to humans, not by humans *to themselves*.

This also means life is a dialogue, not a monologue—an anointing,
not a procedure—an inspiration, not a doctrine. Today's religious
leaders have spoken eloquently "about" God and "to" God. Now it's
time to let God speak too!

Did You See the Gorilla?

So we turn toward authentic, *firsthand* living—we seek the intensity of *sheer* life—we enter a far *larger* "reality"—we plunge into an unknown, yet absolute, *Presence*. . . .

How I wish!

Usually, we walk blindly through the bored humdrum of a day-to-day, take-for-granted world. If we look at life, we look from a distance. If we consider spiritual things, we simply talk or read about them. "If there is a Holy Spirit," we say, "it's certainly not part of 'real life'." As a result, we crowd God's "presence" to the margins. Worse still, we trivialize it or set it aside for "special occasions."

But prophetic awareness is a *different* awareness. It is a "wonderful waiting," a "loud listening," a "ready resting," a "wild patience." Of course, these paradoxical sensations more clearly reflect Scriptural "senses" than the knee-jerk urges of the selfish self. Spiritual senses, for example, disclose the otherworldly difference between merely "hearing" and truly "listening." And, they belong, as well, to a much "bigger" realm—*trans*personal, *trans*cultural, *trans*rational. . . .

In other words, they think "outside the envelope." Here's an example:

In a recent experiment,[10] volunteers were shown a brief basketball film. Before the film, they were told to count how many times one team passed the ball. Then, at the end of the film, they were asked if they saw anything unusual. Most did not. Yet, halfway through the film, a man wearing a gorilla suit walked through the players, beat his chest to the camera, then walked off.

Showing the film again, the reality of the "gorilla" stunned the blindly focused volunteers. For finally, they were forced to think "outside the envelope."

This experiment proves we see what we *expect* to see—and we don't see what we don't expect to see. Again, we are talking about the powerful role of prophetic awareness—or, the lack of it.

A "different" awareness, by the way, doesn't mean a loss of common sense. We still have one foot in this world. We still see the extraordinary *within* the ordinary. And, welcoming this wonder, we *never surrender good reasons* for reason.

No Junk

In prophetic awareness, though, nothing is junk. Anything can catch on fire at any moment. Everything "points." Everything "speaks." Absolutely everything is important and significant.

"The *whole earth* is full of his glory."[11]

So inspired awareness comes to us in any form—and through any awareness of any form. This means the religious artifacts, rituals, and symbols we've constructed are *not* the only mediators to His Presence. In fact, everything—whether secular or sacred—surpasses its appearance. Everything presents a message beyond its medium. Everything serves as a potential metaphor.

What we have wrongly set aside as "art," for example, shows up incognito in life itself—anywhere, any time, and in any form. What a profound opportunity!

When Spirit takes on body and body takes on Spirit—when the "Word becomes flesh," in other words—there is a powerful sense of another world being rendered. At first, we may be stunned beyond belief. But, later, we are stunned *beyond disbelief.* For this is the evidence of "immediate experience"—the same evidence that proves anything and everything.

No *prima donnas*

Obviously, I'm speaking to the leaders of the emerging church. Yet, I must speak for the "sheep" as well as the "shepherds."

The "sheep" languish with gifts even more latent than those of the "shepherds." They're taught, for example, not to compete with "real" spiritual leadership. So they stand in line for their cupful of stale, second-hand spirituality. And, all the while, they suffer this meanspirited paradox:

> . . . a Spirit that is much too obvious to see and much too close to reach.[12]

Yet, God shares His Spirit equally among all sentient beings. There are no *prima donnas* here. Wonder and sacred power are available to all. Sadly, though, these "powers" usually come as carbon copies of someone else's story. And these hand-me-down reports always prove poor substitutes for the "original copy."

Let's face it. Each of us is an active, proactive, creative agent. In other words, we ignite every moment of our history—no matter how big or how small that moment may be. And regardless of our ineptness, God still works through the least of us to accomplish His purpose.

So we count, and what we do counts. The Lord of History places awesome imperatives on those responsible for empowering the "sheep." And this empowerment is far more significant than "getting what's-his-name to read a prayer."

———————— ⸱⸱⸱ ⸱⸱ ● ⸱⸱ ⸱⸱⸱ ————————

If future leaders refuse this responsibility, who will teach the sheep? Who will stake their lives on lived parables—dangerous make-believe—and grace-filled "fictions"? Who will boldly demand the prophetic lifestyles needed in today's prophetic world?

The leaders of the emerging church! There is no one else.

Come join the *real* world—a place where the world's action truly takes place.

Endnotes

1. Leonard Sweet, SoulTsunami: Sink or Swim in the New Millennium Culture," (Grand Rapids, MI: Zondervan, 1999) p. 378.

2. We have long worshiped the great artistic achievements of the ancient Greeks and have blindly put down similar attempts among the ancient Hebrews. A closer, more honest examination of Scripture reveals, however, the Hebrews understood prophetic creativity far more than any culture then or since then.

3. Benjamin Franklyn, Poor Richard's Almanack, 1739.

4. Erich Bridges, "Reaching the 'Oral Majority'" *Bp News*, October, 2004 http://www.bpnews.net/bpnews.asp?ID=19311

5. Hosea 12:10.

6. Hebrews 11:1.

7. William Wordsworth, quoted in Richard Dover, "What is a Poet?" *Lyrical Ballads by William Wordsworth*, May 4, 1995 http://www. newi.ac.uk/rdover/words/ ballads.htm

8. Hebrews 11:1.

9. I Corinthians 7:31.

10. Richard Wiseman, quoted in "Did You Spot the Gorilla?" *Web*

Evangelism Bulletin, August, 2004 http://guide.gospelcom.net/
resources/webull04aug2.php#did_you_spot_the_gorilla_

11. Isaiah 6:3.

12. Ken Wilber, A Theory of Everything: An Integral Vision for
Business, Politics, Science, and Spirituality (Boston: Shambhala,
2000) p 141.

A GREEK "SOUL"

*Hyper*modern and *Super*skeptical

Too many emerging church leaders nurse too many self-decep-
tions. And we find one of the most alarming fallacies in their
"freedom from old ways of thinking." They claim "a radically
different mindset, value system, and worldview",[1] but for most
emerging leaders the facts prove otherwise. They profess craving the
future, but they're still controlled by the past. They talk big about the
"big picture," but they still buy into history's heresies.

Here's an example:

Too many emerging leaders blindly embrace a Greek "Christianity"
where faith is an "idea"—nothing more, nothing less. Like early
Greek theologians, they still filter the Gospel through formula,
analysis, theory and conjecture. Philosophical dialogue, in fact,
defines the movement. In their own words, truth is "a complex
philosophical, epistemological question."[2]

Perhaps we shouldn't blame them. After all, modernity has always
been more Greek than Christian. (Consider, for example, our college
curricula.) Yet, we *must* blame them, for the emerging church claims
to be "*post*modern." Indeed, the movement exists *primarily* to
protest modernism!

So how can its leaders avoid the fact they are more modern than
postmodern? How can they avoid the reality they are even *hyper*-
modern? And, how can they avoid the naked truth of an "enlightened" learning that is not only "skeptical" but *super*skeptical?

In other words, how can they go on blindly squeezing the last drop of
blood out of already dead cadavers.

Future historians will surely call this a "scandal."

Emerging church leaders frequently use modern thinking, for example, to criticize modern thinking. They often parade effective language to communicate the ineffectiveness of language. And, they even manipulate others against the deceit of being manipulated by others.

Only their style is different.

Yet, this mess emerges from more than modernity. For our ancient Greek legacy is totally incompatible with the ancient Hebrews. Greek minds and Hebraic consciousness held vastly different realities. Nowhere, for example, does Scripture get even close to a philosophical discussion.

So with our Greek "knowing," we've lost Hebrew "knowing"—with our knowledge "about" God, we've lost knowledge "of" God—with our disclosure of God, we've lost God's disclosure to us. With our cold abstractions, we've lost lived moments—with our "ahistorical" God, we've lost the Lord of History—and with our right "thinking," we've lost right "living."

With our Greek God of "fate," we no longer have the Hebrew God of faith—with our impersonal God, we no longer have a personal God—with our passive faith, we no longer have a proactive faith.

With our disembodied wisdom, we no longer have embodied wisdom—with our refusal of feelings, we no longer have felt meanings—and with our theological systems, we no longer have paradox, enigma, or the significance of signs.

In short, the bending of the Gospel into a Greek world is the story of Western Christianity. And, within this story, our Greek "souls" have solemnly preserved our racial amnesia—our collective unconscious.

"Isn't it wonderful that God is just like us?"

Yet, these wrong assumptions happen at the wrong moment. For an old structure of knowledge is fading, and its emerging "Greek" leaders are fading with it. In a massive shift, ancient epistemology and classical theology are being left behind. Already, we live in an age of theological "anarchy," and an altered future won't make sense even to the anarchists!

All of us parade this fallacy. But the tools that achieved results in the last era will not attain results in the next era. In other words, we won't be able to drag modernity into the postmodern world. The passive words of "pure" spectators—the logical, linear rules of academic "think tanks"—and the theological veracity of cold and calculating brains will never pass the inevitable baggage screens.

The future belongs to a new way of thinking, a new way of knowing what we know. It will return us to an oral culture—or rather, an electronic oral culture. Creativity, artistry, and empathy—metaphor, meaning, and emotion—pattern, synthesis, and the big picture will prove the *lingua franca* of the future. Spontaneity, fluidity, and open-endedness will release its revelations. And, its empowered "words" will actually "do things"—will anticipate and summon things—will break into the present and transform things.

In short, we will no longer be "thinking" in the usual sense of the word. For the new spirituality is "unthinkable." Instead, we will be projecting a new world.

Endnotes

1. Andrew Jones, quoted in Tim Conder, *The Church in Transition: The Journey of Existing Churches in the Emerging Culture* (Grand Rapids, MI; Zondervan, 2006) pp 22, 25.

2. Tony Jones, quoted in Peter Walker and Tyler Clark, "Missing the Point?" *Relevant Magazine*, Issue 21, July-August, 2006, pp 70-74.

The Friend That Stayed Too Long

Yet, we remain embarrassingly gullible! We either sell out to our insular culture or buy into any historical heresy. We either hustle our cocksure bias or fall for any bogus spirituality.

All of us!

But the Lord of History has confronted our gullibility. All the questionable "tools" we've used to "prove" religious "truth" are being challenged by the unchurched world. For years, churches made "offers that nobody could refuse," but now, the nobodies are refusing those offers.

"Disallowed" knowledge is exciting the unchurched but upsetting the churched. "Realities" supposedly controlled by the church are now controlling the church. And, faded "litmus tests" that "proved" who was the most "religious" are now being "disproved."

It's no surprise, then, that Christian orthodoxy is totally at risk. Right or wrong, our creeds are like sand castles being swept away by the tide. Yet, few admit this scandal. Nobody's asking what's slipping away. And nobody's asking why.

A Conspiracy of a Conspiracy

What's behind all this? What are the historical juggernauts destroying Christian doctrine? And, who are the malicious attackers driving a wedge between the church and its canon?

Could it be bold books and movies like *The Da Vinci Code*? This hoax concocts a conspiracy that hides the supposed marriage between

Jesus and Mary Magdalene. This book spills over with "facts" and "scholarship," but it is mostly fiction and "wildly misinterprets" early Christianity.[1]

In short, it is "a murder mystery masquerading as historical truth."[2]

Already, 44 other books try to correct these lies, but a biblically illiterate public still refuses the church any benefit of the doubt. Indeed, most readers of the *"Code"* revel in its "personal spiritual growth and understanding."[3]

Even religious scholars welcome the book and movie! "Most of the time nobody pays any attention to what we do . . . (but we're gladly) in demand right now."[4] Further, these stories will "give us more tolerance for diverse opinions about Jesus."[5] In other words, "It doesn't matter if it differs from Scripture and biblical history as long as we're having fun."

This novel and blockbuster movie represent full frontal attacks on Christian orthodoxy. They resemble the "gnostic" heresies of early Christianity. Recent discoveries of ancient gnostic gospels, for example, remind us of those who claimed "special knowledge" of things "superior" to Christianity. And the faithless studies of today's excited scholars simply compound these heresies.

Yes, media like *The Da Vinci Code* seem like tsunamis. But they are only ripples on the vast ocean of a dangerous journey.

Surrogate Spiritualities

Even before such attacks, a new secular spirituality was ignoring institutional "authority" and rejecting "absolute truth." Even before such blasphemies, an out-of-church "faith" was repackaging itself into alternative spiritual currents and prevailing as the fastest growing "preference" in popular culture.

In other words, people were meeting God "on their own." Often, spirit-led passions, felt meanings, and out-of-the-blue transformations touched a deeper call. It was enough in itself. It needed no "added glory," it needed no justifying doctrine.

Of course, it could also prove shamefully shallow. And, we see that shallowness in the fringe pop styles of a fragmented culture and in the "pop religions" of a "religion-lite" culture. Obviously, these unmapped mysticisms provide no "anchors"—no accountabilities—no validations—no verifications. . . .

In other words, anything goes!

In worst cases, the knee-jerk "spiritualities" and unredeemed passions of self-interest, self-centeredness, self-preservation, and self-pleasure can overwhelm us. And the seductions of the Other World can evoke the demons of half-truths and half-lies. As a result, surrogate spiritualities can blur the boundaries between cult and culture. And bogus bliss can provoke the re-emergence of a pagan world.

No doubt, the heart of this matter is a matter of the heart. But, somewhere, we hear a cry for integrity.

Alternative "Worlds"

Technology plays the same anything-goes game. It has left veritable reality for Virtual Reality. Virtual Reality (or "VR") has become an alternative world—a reality beyond reality—a simulation beyond simulation. A hyper-reality! We see it in "war games," video games, and flight simulators. We see it in fantasy lands like Las Vegas. And, we see it in sensory experiences that even Mother Nature hasn't experienced.

But VR, in itself, is not bad. After all, all the arts are "virtual"—in other words, they represent things that are not there. And, if we could say that VR, art, and metaphor are virtual synonyms, then we may be "virtual" too. For we're living these things. They're life itself!

Need more endorsement? Then consider this: Judeo-Christian faith speaks of "nonexistent things . . . as if they [already] existed" and gives form to the "substance," "evidence" and "proof" of things we do not see.[6] If that isn't Virtual Reality—at the supernatural level!—then why not?

Still, seraph and snake live side by side in the world of VR. So let the "buyer beware." It's a fluid, ephemeral world where virtual reality and veritable reality overlap. So-called "evidence" might be a simulation itself—or a simulation of a simulation of a simulation. . . .

Anything and everything can be an "authentic fake"[7]—a land of malicious make-believe—a dominion of demons' dreams—a beguiling, captivating, and enthralling fool's paradise. And, as reality becomes less and less important, sensory addicts live more and more for simulated stimuli—no sense of right from wrong, no accountability, and no responsibility.

And, when their simulated senses wear off—when their "fulfillment" remains unfulfilled—when their satisfaction stays unsatisfied, they're right back where they started: needing another "fix."

So VR "travelers" had better "pack" carefully. And, sooner or later, they had better come home. "Coming home" means coming back to all those things that hold us together—all those things that keep us from going crazy—all those "convictions," "credences," and "creeds" the world would rather we not have.

We've got to do better, surely, than the scientist who wore snow shoes once he realized he was standing on literally **nothing**.

A Seldom Told Story

Yet, none of the above suspects have proven the *real* enemy of church doctrine. Books, movies, secular spirituality, and virtual reality may resemble Monsters, Inc., but they're not the main problem. So let's tell a seldom told story:

The early church was vernal and vulnerable. And attacks of heretical teachings (like Gnosticism) forced crises of identity—even of survival! The only help came from Greek/Roman intellectuals[8] who insisted on a strict canon of Scripture.

They were the first to shape Christian doctrine. Thank goodness for their help!

But Greek philosophy became "the friend that stayed too long." Increasingly, its philosophers pulled Scripture through the only world-view they knew. They took the basic phrases of Scripture and molded them into a systematic and philosophical whole. They fed "existence" and "truth" through the filter of formula, analysis, theory and conjecture. . . .

In short, they brought classical rhetoric to the aid of an imperiled religion.

But these well-meaning friends also brought a twice-removed "Good News," a distant "idea" of God, and a disembodied spirit. Christian passions, for example, were considered "ungodly," a "sign of weakness," even a "source of evil." And, anything beyond explana-tion—"mystery," as example—was simply not part of the equation.

Faith was reduced to the intellectual assent and "sacred" integrity of the logical mind.

This bending of Scripture into a Greek world is the story of Western Christianity. And, today, nothing has changed. We remain more

Greek than Judeo-Christian. And our Greek view is "the very essence of how we know, or can be certain, about what is true and false."[9]

It's the story of a Greek "soul". . . .

. . . and it continues the story of the emerging church movement.

Where the Rubber Hits the Road

Shouldn't the obvious be obvious? Shouldn't the emerging church know these things?

Incredibly, we don't.

Greek world views and Hebrew realities were dissonantly different. Greek minds and Hebraic consciousness were profoundly incompatible. Scripture doesn't even consider philosophical discussions. And when Jesus said, "I am the truth," His truth has nothing to do with a logical or systematic theology.

Clearly, the Hebrews knew a different knowing. They grasped unspoken revelations suddenly and intuitively. They embraced understandings that come from *only* "the spirit in a man"—from *only* "the breath of the Almighty."[10] And, these understandings were more than "ideas." After all, "What is born of the Spirit *is Spirit*."[11]

So Paul's warning should come as no surprise: "Reason without the Holy Spirit . . . *is death*."[12]

For this Spirit is not a "theological Spirit." Rather than the cold abstractions of a remote and unchanging God, biblical writers encountered the Spirit in *every* living and changing event. Rather than theoretical doctrines devoid of real-life evidence, Hebrew believers found the Spirit in *all* personal encounters—even the chaos and mess that follow fallen people in a fallen world.

Their "theology" was "where the rubber hits the road."

Rather than a stoic apathy and a disembodied wisdom, Hebrew prophets knew a guileless sympathy and an embodied wisdom. Rather than a cold journey from doctrine to decision, Hebrew hearts moved from passions to prophecy.

Their feelings and thoughts were the same!

Again, this Truth was an *embodied* Truth. And, for that purpose, they shared heightened sensitivities to "felt meanings"—visceral feelings, heartfelt emotions, ecstatic passions. Yet, these feelings were not "flaky"—nor were they merely subjective! For the Hebrews discerned the difference between survival biology (what they called the "flesh") and aesthetic wisdom (what they called the "spirit").

Without doubt, they recognized the wasteful and destructive passions of common selfishness—all the phony bliss that points away from God. But, they also recognized inspired revelations and felt meanings that were far more than just "feelings." For these feelings bridged the sensuous and spiritual worlds—much the way we experience profound beauty today. In those moments, passions, paradox, and parables became one—a transcendent transparency that points only to God.

In short, biblical writers offered self-evident signs and self-authenticating tests of the vast differences between "flesh" and "spirit." Though our modern "idea" of faith considers all "feelings" a sign of weakness, the Hebrews knew redeemed passions as their source of strength.

Yet, their passions were not passive. Their promptings remained, instead, powerful motives, flexed "springs," and triggered "implosions" that could empower every moment, act, and deed. The focus of their faith, in other words, was the "doing" of their faith where the whole of life becomes hallowed.

Nothing was a mere "idea"—nothing was a cold calculation—and nothing was too profane or too trivial.

Clearly, these believers *participated* with the Lord of History. And their participation was more than mythology, more than theology. Their very destiny was bound up in the moment by moment manifestations of history. Every action birthed ultimate meanings. Every action launched eternal significance.

It was a *reciprocal* relationship—a dynamic reality—a historical drama. It transcended the separation of man from God. It was the union of eternity and history.

No Place to Go

What, then, will we do with our Greek friends? Beyond doubt, they fathered our culture!

Yes, the Nicene Creed is beautiful, and I confess it repeatedly. Yes, the Doctrine of the Trinity is profound, and I welcome its profundity. But nowhere in Scripture can we find a philosophical discussion of the Godhead. And, nowhere in Scripture can we find a 3-part "system" within this Godhead.

That's OK. Our long heritage of fussy theological argument doesn't bother me. I can even live with some of the sad distortions, schismatic dogmas, and stale codes.

What bothers me is what's *left out*—the terrible omissions of Christianity's *intended themes*. When we replace Scripture with books "about" Scripture—when we prefer the "higher" goals of official systems, rational structures, and stored facts—and, when we limit our "revelation" to proposed ideas, ordained thoughts, or intellectual assent, we lose something far more precious than what we've gained.

We've almost completely lost, for example, the Hebrew notion of "Spirit." For Spirit moves beyond static dogmas. Intuitive visions outrun legal reasonings. And, personal revelations lead beyond official doctrines.

Plainly, no theology can disclose God's Self-disclosure. No reason can reveal what reason alone cannot grasp. And, no intellect can analyze Something that transcends analysis. Again, our "theology of the Spirit" does not even come close to Paul's "demonstration of the Spirit."[13]

As a result, we've lost the prophetic power of communion and creativity.

And, that's not all. We've also lost life's mission. Creeds that talk only about right "thinking" conveniently avoid right "living"—raw discipleship—and *incarnate* lives. And, passive doctrines that push only theological correctness totally ignore personal actions and the ultimate meanings of our actions.

We "get our ticket punched," but then we have no place to go.

When we remove an abstract God from history, we reject the Lord of History. And, without the Lord of History, we're left with an aloof and indifferent God who leaves us nothing but "fate"—immutable and impersonal. No wonder the church can't figure out what to do, for fate was the ultimate idea and ultimate destiny of our Greek fore-fathers.

Then, obviously, our great theological "achievements" neglect life itself. For the Greeks tried feverishly to "cleanse" God of the mud of man, the filth of history, and the "flesh" of Jesus. That's the reason their doctrinal "absolutes" embraced "thinking" to the determined exclusion of "doing" and "being." And, they cut life even further out of the picture with their needless schism between the "sacred" and the "secular."

So the very things Scripture mentions most remain missing in today's Christendom.

Why can't we see this? Because our culture has become a racial amnesia—an illusory history—a collective unconscious. And, inevitably, we get drunk on ethnic pride and a God created in our own image.

As a result, Christendom is losing its influence. And our Christian "apologists"—religious "persuaders"—are becoming increasingly known for their insincere techniques and weighted agendas.

In 1966, the world announced that "God is Dead." Now we know what's really dead.

> "Don't become so well-adjusted to
> your culture that you fit into it without
> even thinking."[14]

Falling in Love With *Love*

Ironically, the postmodern world needs orthodoxy more than ever. With in-your-face heresy and anything-goes spirituality, the world is getting "curiouser and curiouser." So already we hear a cry for "Truth" with a capital "T," an unspoken plea for bedrock foundations, and an openness toward new and radical "orthodoxies."

Caught among such forces, history proves that our theology *will change*. Today's conflict mirrors, for example, the same forces that confronted the Second Century church. Then and now, a crisis of identity and the urgency of survival demands our attention.

We've got to get it right!

"Getting it right" requires a new integrity of the Spirit. We must learn, for example, the difference between a craftsman and an anointed artist—dazzling skill and a moment of true power—the intelligence of the mind and the wisdom of the heart. And, within this new integrity, we must learn the difference between doctrines and inspirations—monologues and dialogues—procedures and anointings.

Yes, the Word will always remain the Word, but we will find a new "substance," "evidence," and "proof" for the Word.[15] And, along the way, we won't need to parody ancient Hebrew culture—we won't need to re-Hebraize Christianity. We will rediscover, instead, the pristine Truth *within* a former culture.

Will there be a place for scholars? For doctrines? For orthodoxy? It certainly seems so! For we still need informed honesty and disciplined scholarship. We still need to understand what we've understood. We still need the secure comforts of a grounded knowing.

Yet, something new is happening. We are rethinking thinking. We are discovering new ways of meaning what we mean and new ways of signifying what is significant. For the first time in history we are being offered the integrity of the spirit as well as the integrity of the mind—a *combined* excellence with new credibilities and more profound certainties.

Hopefully, we will get beyond our built-in embarrassments and finally discover that insight always comes before insightful opinions—that aesthetic truth always emerges before conceptual truth—and that the "wisdom of the heart" always precedes the intelligence of the mind.

Yes, we will always need a balance between "orthopraxy" and "orthodoxy"—between faithful "flowings" in the Holy Spirit and mature underpinnings of the Holy Spirit. But we must still return to our Source, over and over. . . . In other words, we can only comprehend when we are comprehended.

Does this mean that "doctrine" and "orthodoxy" are not quite the right terms? Maybe so.

In the meantime, today's scholars will continue their search for integrity. They will find new ways to speak credibly about the incredible. They will point with new boldness to the veracities of their experiences. And—in their piercing discernments—they will finally fall in love with Love.

————— ∞∞●∞∞ —————

This Spirit-birthed age is birthing new spirit! It's a creative mutation driven by God. It's not a doomsday, it's a divine deliverance.

We are being "reintroduced" to God.

> "Whoever marries the spirit of this age
> will find himself a widower in the
> next."[16]

Endnotes

1. Dr. Harold Attridge, Dean of Yale's Divinity School, quoted in Stephen Shields, "The Da Vinci Code and a Hunger for Something More," *Next-Wave Ezine*, May, 2006   http://www.the-next-wave -ezine.info/issue 89/index.cfm?id=12&ref=COVERSTORY

2. Sandra Miesel, "Da Duh Vinci Code" *TotheSource Newsletter*, May 3, 2006, http://www.tothesource .org/5_3_2006/5_3_2006.htm

3. Last year, pollster George Barna reported that 53 percent of U.S. adults who finished the book said it had been helpful in their "personal spiritual growth and understanding."

4. Gail Streete, quoted in Jeffrey Weiss, "Scholars debunk facts in a work of fiction," *Seattle Times, May 13, 2006* http://archives.seattle times.nwsource .com/

5. From an interview on National Public Radio.

6. Romans 4:17, *New International Version & The Amplified Bible*; Isaiah 46:10, *The Amplified Bible*; Hebrews 11:1, *King James Bible & The Amplified Bible*.

7. Umberto Eco, quoted in "Hyperreality," *Wikipedia*, Dec., 2006 http://en.wikipedia.org/wiki/Hyperreality

8. Early examples include Irenaeus of Lyons (ca. 130-200) and Tertullian (ca. 160-225).

9. John H. Armstrong, "How Important is Propositional Truth?" *Advancing the Christian Tradition in the 3rd Millennium*, March 18, 2006 http://johnharmstrong.typepad.com/john_h_armstrong_/2006/03/how_important_i.html

10. Job 32:8, *New International Version*.

11. John 3:6, *The Amplified Bible*.

12. Romans 8:6,7; *The Amplified Bible*.

13. I Corinthians 2:4, *The Amplified Bible*.

14. Romans 12:1, 2; The Message Bible.

15. The definition of "faith." Hebrews 11:1.

16. William Inge, quoted in Dick Staub, "Ancient Faith. Pop Faith." *Culture Watch*, May 15, 2006 http://www.dickstaub.com/culturewatch.php?record_id=1014

"We're Not in Kansas Anymore"

By now, it should be obvious that something big is happening. Bigger than what we're doing. Bigger than what we're predicting. We can't see where it's leading us, but we can certainly see "We're not in Kansas anymore". . . .

. . . or in "Christendom."

We recognize this larger-than-life moment when something "other-than-us" precipitates things, when catalytic events cause seismic shifts, when outside forces drive history's "quickenings." We recognize this colossal revelation when spiritual certainty turns uncertain, when it spirals out of control, when the spirituality we supposedly "controlled" now controls us.

We recognize this intrusive Otherness when moving events race forward at breathless speed, when multiple "tipping points" tumble headlong into the future, when the cascading rapids of change catch us by surprise. We recognize it when quixotic events move evermore quickly, when the rate of change accelerates, when our "feedback" loops compound their own force.

"So what?"—the oblivious say. "Change is always with us." And true enough. Yet today, the *dynamics* of change have changed. Normal "change" has become abnormal, linear change has become exponential, and expected change has turned unexpected.

In short, we know something big is happening when reality moves beyond our understanding, when "knowing" is repeatedly overthrown, when the fabric of faith feels ruptured. We see it when conventional models of the future become irrelevant, when "event horizons" lie beyond our ability to predict, when hidden goals seem like "black holes"—refusing further light.

In other words, we're rapidly approaching a time when the church—as we know it—cannot continue. We are arriving at a moment from which the illusions of the present can never return. We are facing an "essential strangeness" beyond which this era will end.

It is the end of something and the beginning of something totally Other—a transformation or creative mutation of spirituality itself.

> "See! I have set before you a door
> wide open which no one is able to
> shut."[1]

"Rare and Momentous"

These stark facts are not science fiction. They are not the pastimes of "end times," where fear and hope struggle for market supremacy. They are not the sectarian skirmishes of a "Second Reformation." Nor do they represent "rapture for nerds" or "grace for geeks."

And, contrary to opinion, these mutations are not the "latest and greatest" church rages. They are not "official" renewals, "just right" public policies or the pastors' favorite programs. They are not mere "improvements" in the way we "do church." And, they are not the reworking of the past into the same untenable models.

For these historic transformations are larger than our sellout to show-business or our caricature of culture. They are larger than our accommodation to kids or their morphing of "cool" into a religion. And, they are larger than the "largest" of the churches or the latest list of God's "chosen."

These looming events lie beyond even a "thinking man's guide to the future"—newly invented social theories—or the next academic "think tank."

After all, all such efforts are "deja vu all over again"[2]—the continued, dreary rehearsal of Christendom's failed glories.

Still, the epochal phenomena that lie beyond us are not "pie-in-the-sky" stuff. They're right here—right now. What's happening to the church is what we can see happening. And, what's happening reflects the actual world. Yet, it also reflects the world as it *will be*—a world far more real than the present world which, even now, is "passing away."[3]

It is "a rare and momentous alignment of forces."[4] It is "the glow that suffuses everything here in the dawn of an expected new day."[5]

"I am . . . He . . . Who is to come."[6]

The Fault Line of the Future

So, then, what do we see happening that confirms this Happening? What do we know that confirms this Knowing?

To begin, our "thinking"—or, more to the point, the *way* we think—is changing. And—as a result—the *way* we believe is changing. That belief, of course, is not a different "Word," it's a different understanding of the Word. For spirituality is converting to new sympathies. Faith is transmuting to new sensitivities. And this Spirit-birthed age is birthing new spirit!

Consider where we've been: We've journeyed from farms, to factories, to "information." The agricultural and industrial ages were built on people's backs. And the Information Age was built on people's brains—logical and precise.

The future, though, no longer belongs to cold and calculating brains—the guys who know only "sequence," "literalness," and "analysis." As mentioned earlier, it belongs, instead, to creativity, artistry, and empathy—metaphor, meaning, and emotion—pattern, synthesis, and the big picture.

It belongs to those who crave a *different* beauty—a *postmodern* beauty—a *virtual (yet more real)* beauty.

Today, it is their "thinking" that matters most. Their yearning marks the fault line between those who get ahead and those who fall behind—those who win and those who lose—those who innovate and those who stagnate.

Even church leaders are "thinking" differently. What was once a "subculture" is now mainstream. What was once embarrassing is now respectable. What was once powerless is now empowered. For once again, "spiritual" leaders are allowing a Sovereign Spirit to speak through their "spirit-filled" spirits.

This new spirituality may reflect Christianity, but not "Christendom." It may reflect the Hebrews, but not the Greeks. And, it may reflect the first century, but not the twenty-first century.

In Cahoots

Such epiphanies already shock "enlightened" civilization. Yet, the "magic" of technology and the "miracles" of modern physics will soon overwhelm even common sense. Science and the supernatural, it seems, are increasingly in cahoots. And we've missed it because we've seen only the warm-up act.

When church leaders finally grasp the amazing implications, the "proof" of ancient Scripture will change dramatically. No longer will we hide behind the worn out dogmas of the past—doctrines that are only "believed" and can never be "lived."

New forces—both sensuous and caring—are already blending the scientific with the senses, technology with touch, and the Internet with intimacy. And, fearfully, we'll even reshape life through genetic manipulation, we'll remold matter through nanotechnology, and we'll recast consciousness through super-intelligent machines.

As if this isn't supernatural enough, embarrassed physicists now admit that a miraculous realm exists within this realm. They confess an "Other World" within this world. And, they claim a prophetic power within a commonplace power.

Take quantum physics as example: In the odd world of quantum, things exist in a multitude of states until tipped toward a definite outcome by our "participation." It's impossible, for example, to look at a quantum event without changing it. There's an unavoidable bond, in other words, between the observer and the world observed.

So we are participants more than spectators. We are coauthors more than bystanders. Our world is more a "Creating" than a "Creation." In other words, our "desire reveals design, and (our) design reveals destiny."[7]

The quantum world promises we can "make the Holy Spirit offers He can't refuse." And Jesus made the same promise.[8]

A New Empowerment of Faith

This discovery would not have surprised the early Hebrews. They knew all things exist in the invisible realm before they appear in the visible realm. That's the reason Hebrew faith was the "substance"—or raw material—of which things were made.[9] They simply copied the example of God who spoke "of nonexistent things . . . as if they [already] existed"—"declaring the end and the result from the beginning."[10]

It was not unusual, in other words, that under dry skies, Elijah announces, "There is the sound of abundance of rain." Nor was it rare when Jesus declared, "I have overcome the world," when—in reality—His victory became fact when He later died and rose again.

Of course, the spiritual implications of modern physics are enormous.[11] When our decisions and God's will mutually move each other, the role of divine action takes on totally new meaning. The Church must learn to embolden these understandings in a new empowerment of faith.

The world of invisible forces is more real than reality itself. Today, our imagination is being baptized, and our windows on God's miraculous presence are reopening. Our "thinking" is no longer bound to an ancient Greek world. . . .

. . . we are projecting a new world.[12]

Endnotes

1. Revelation 3:8, *The Amplified Bible*.

2. Attributed to Yoggi Berra.

3. I Corinthians 7:31, *The Amplified Bible*.

4. Steven Johnson, *Interface Culture: How New Technology Transforms the Way We Create and Communicate* (New York: Basic Books, 1997) p 187.

5. Jürgen Moltmann, quoted in Grenz and Franke, *Beyond Foundationalism: Shaping Theology In A Postmodern Context* (Louisville: Westminster John Knox Press, 2001) p. 239.

6. Revelation 1:8, *The Amplified Bible*.

7. John Eldredge, *Wild at Heart: Discovering the Secret of a Man's Soul* (Nashville: Thomas Nelson Publishers, 2001) p. 48.

8. Matthew 17:20.

9. Hebrews 11:1.

10. Romans 4:17, Isaiah 46:10; *The Amplified Bible.*

11. We include other theories as well—especially "string theory."

12. William Irwin Thompson, *Coming Into Being* (New York: St. Martin's Press, 1996) p. 73.

A DESIGNER DELIVERANCE

Old-fashioned Salvations

Everything—and I do mean "everything"—has gone out of style! The old-fashioned notions of "getting religion"—including repentance, redemption, deliverance, salvation, and being "born again," belong to the past. Emerging leaders may talk on and on about the "conversion" of the church but they rarely talk about the conversion of the unchurched.

Yet, who can blame them?

Increasingly, our salvation "system" reflects the triumph of man, where "scoring" feeds the hungry pride of those who "do the saving." Prepackaged programs, for example, control the conversions while cookie-cutter salvations secure the quantities. Never mind that man has never saved *anyone*. And, never mind that God has *already* done the saving.

Yet, this "system" has become a means to an end. "If it works, do it." Some clergy, for example, win more converts by fear than by joy. That is, they win more converts by sin than by grace. Other clergy promote an easily marketed "benefit plan" that guarantees health and wealth and prevents suffering and sorrow.

Whatever the strategy, these clergy always throw in a few "extra" rules. They insist that the "unsaved" must "do what it takes" to become a Christian. And "doing what it takes" means the "lost" must lift themselves to heaven with the right "bootstraps." So new recruits must hear a tedious recital of cultural mores, morals, and manners. And they must hear a repeated litany of precise taboos, conventions, and virtues.

Then—after it's all over—the "saved" usually live no differently than the "unsaved." They may be "converts," but they are seldom "disciples."

"Salvations in the Sauna"

A far different ploy, however, arises from the more "sophisti-cated"—or "educated"—clergy. Those "in the know" have reduced salvation to a "thinking man's religion"—salvation by informa-tion—deliverance by data. These "keepers of the creeds" invoke centuries of rhetoric in winning reasoned agreement with their *proposed* ideas about God.

Of course, "knowing" something was never the same as living it. And, regardless of the "method," manipulation for a divine end always proves a contradiction.

So we see why many emerging church leaders avoid the whole salvation issue! In its place, they offer a "relaxed" repentance, a "designer" deliverance, a "cool" salvation, a "multiple choice" belief. . . . In other words, "Just hang out with us and enjoy 'salvation in the sauna'."

Such confused conversions totally ignore hidden dishonesties, messed up lives, and single-minded selfishness. (We used to call this "sin," but most emerging leaders are too "sophisticated" for that.) And the notion of being spiritually dead—though mentally alert—does not cross their minds. In fact, "It's not even a possibil-ity."

While we're at it, don't mention the word "evil." Such a notion is "a naive holdover from primitive mentalities." Today's "enlightened" leaders now classify this ancient term as a mere "absence of good" or—in worst cases—a "temporary illness."

Such indifference to our spiritual deformities makes "goodness" meaningless. It makes profoundly changed hearts and the integrity that flows from changed hearts not worth talking about. And, today's emerging leaders might as well forget the Gospel. After all, Jesus called his followers to change themselves first. . . .

. . . then the world.

A New "Altar Call"

Yet, the Lord of History has changed history, so "changing the world" must take place within a changed world. For example, no one in today's world—including the Holy Spirit—likes steamroller religion, in-your-face salvations, or hit-and-run evangelism. No one knowingly suffers manipulators, con artists, or any-means-to-an-end evangelists. And no one honestly prefers the rhetoric, jargon, and formulas of antiquated institutions.

In short, the world has refused loveless Christianity. The un-churched, for example, have refused the big egos behind "big evangelism." And, the discerning have refused "quantity" as a deceitful substitute for "quality."

So emerging church leaders must seek a new "altar call," a new "salvation," a new "evangelism"—a new honesty, a new authenticity, a new reverence for the Mystery—a new caring, a new belonging, and a new journeying. . . .

. . . yes, it's a journeying, a maturing, a growing. It's not just a one-time event!

So the new evangelism will look more like "planting" and "water-ing," mentoring and modeling through endless stages of growth. The goal, in other words, is not salvation. The goal is discipleship. Jesus said, "Watch me, then you do it." And, finally, "Go teach others."

What's our problem?

Where Are the Disciples?

We can no longer ignore the hidden facts. Our whole value system is shifting to suit the needs of individuals. Our entire social structure is reshaping to serve the passions of its participants. On a massive magnitude, the global world is reapportioning power from the "somebodies" to the "nobodies."

These facts forecast a transfigured "laity," and the emerging church will not escape the implications.

Spirituality now encompasses more than "church." Christ's mission now embraces more than "religion." For spiritual leaders are showing up outside the established church, and "unbelievers" are becoming "believers" outside our sacred "systems."

At the same time, we see an unprecedented transfer of divine power from the ordained to the ordinary, from the educated to the uneducated, from the empowered to the unempowered. God is breaking the constraints, in other words, on who and what a spiritual leader is. Spiritual "somebodies" are being redefined, and the significance for emerging church leaders is enormous.

New Players on The Playing Field

Emerging churches talk big about each member having a "ministry"—about the importance of the "laity"—about the "priesthood of all believers." For most churches, though, nothing has changed. The old English word *laite* (or "laity") still means the same: It means *everybody else*—the "un-clergy," the "un-ordained," the "un-empowered," the "un-emerging." Or, we could call them the "Sunday spectators," the "churchgoers," the "religious crowd". . . .

. . . in other words, all those one step removed from God.

But behind the scenes, a new laity emerges. They are spiritually yearning—yet institutionally alienated—trailblazers. They are often the unwashed, unwanted, and unrefined. Or, more to the point, they are "not-us." They are "alien" believers no longer satisfied to be marginalized, to be excluded, or to simply support someone else's program.

They are leaving their spectator seats, and they are refusing yesterday's "manna."

Of course, these believers still need belonging, and they still need redemption. Most of all, though, they need *empowerment*. They're tired of old illusions. They want a *true* "priesthood of every believer." And, they want a *totally* new relation between the dispensers and receivers of sacred information.

In short, they want a new way of thinking.

And they won't wait. Already, they're finding ministries beyond the religious sector. They're discovering the power of widespread, creative networking. They're taking their place as players on the playing field. In other words, they're becoming inspired participants in the *real* world.

Though we may refuse the idea, they are Christ's brothers and sisters. They are ordinary people doing extraordinary things. And, they are leading Christianity into lands where old maps no longer work.

John Wesley is hidden in their DNA. Wesley said if a person's heart is in the right place and they are obedient to the Lord, he cares

> not a straw whether they be clergy or laymen. (For) such alone will shake the gates of hell and set up the Kingdom of Heaven on earth.[1]

The True Story

Today, we're forced to admit our idea of "laity" was never the intention of the early church. To say "laity" (or *laos* in the New Testament) was simply to say "Christian." In other words, the laity were not a subspecies of ***anything***.[2]

Free and spontaneous worship gave central place to *all* participants. "Spiritual leadership," in fact, was widely shared. Lydia and Onesimus, for example, did the work of "pastors," yet they were not "clergy." Indeed, they may not have been even members of a "church."

And, though we may not believe it, men and women shared equally in praying and prophesying.[3] And society's outcasts—rebels (Simon), fanatics (Paul), thieves (Onesimus), corrupt officials (Matthew), and worse—were the leading saints of the early church.

It was only later that Ignatius and Clement argued for the dividing of "clergy" and "laity"—the severing of superiors and subordinates. After the first disciples, however, the power of the church came not from the hierarchy. It came from the monastic movement—ordinary believers who turned their back on an increasingly secular church to seek God above all things.

Let's face it. The monastic movement saved the church!

But history repeats itself. So, once again, shamed believers like Martin Luther complained,

> . . . it is pure invention that pope, bishop, priests, and monks are called the spiritual estate, and all princes, lords, artisans, and farmers are called the temporal estate. This is indeed a piece of deceit and hypocrisy.[4]

What's-His-Name

Yet, nothing has changed—even in most "emerging churches." Today's church is still a "Christendom" church—a centuries-old legacy of the Roman Empire. It ignores the signs of the times—the raw truths of a *pre*-Christendom heritage and the sober warnings of a *post*-Christendom reality. It has become irrelevant to the Lord of History.

"Christendom" churches restrict things "religious" to certain times, certain places, certain people—"sacred" programs, "sacred" pews, "sacred" privileges. . . . Their little "kingdoms" are their only community, and their little communities are their only "calling." So their very existence requires pulling people in and never letting them go.

It's a survival anxiety, a maintenance mentality.

In Christendom churches, all "religious" energies must be focused toward the church. That means "professional" Christians must get the "amateur" Christians to "fill all the slots." That means a command-and-control structure must prompt a silent consensus to work all the in-house programs.

It's a closed system, of course, with lockstep procedures, fixed agendas, and authorized leaders. So spirit-led laity and creative self-starters need not apply. And all the others must never stray from official guidelines

God help you if you make a mistake.

Obviously, these churches invest more in programs than in people. And, when necessary, they are ready to sacrifice people on behalf of their "first love." In other words, if you've not chosen your own cross, they are more than happy to choose one for you.

And like most wars, "the soldiers are expendable."

It's no surprise that Christian "movers and shakers" *outside* the church feel totally underutilized—totally out of the loop. They're told, for example, "Put your dream on hold and come support a *real* ministry." That "real" ministry, however, turns out to be a frustrated club of part-time, spiritual dilettantes. And the clergy respond to their inevitable complaints by "getting what's-his-name to read a prayer."

And they ask, "Where are the disciples?"

But pity most the multitudes of hand-fed sheep—the passive churchgoers blindly following out of habit or duty. Or grieve especially for those lethargic conformers already seduced by the addictive consumer church. Long ago, someone higher up decided these laity were "needy"—that they must be taken care of—that they must be given carbon copies, hand-me-down reports, of someone else's story.

Yet, each of us is a creative being. Each of us touches off our moment in history—no matter how big or how small that moment may be. And, regardless of our ineptness, God still works through each of us to accomplish His purpose.

> "There is anger over the hogging of ministry by professionals; anger over not empowering all Christians for ministry; anger over not releasing the spiritual potential in every believer."[5]

A Team of "Spiritual Entrepreneurs"

But angry believers won't have long to wait. The old notion of "professional Christians" is now questioned. For today, a new synergy—a horizontal synergy—is emerging between the leaders and the led.

Already, authentic leaders are changing from harvesting to cultivating, from manipulating to mentoring, from teaching to modeling. Already, they are changing from programs to people, from "doing" ministry to "equipping" ministry, from managing institutions to making disciples.

Of course, the secular world had already discovered this shift from "hierarchical, competitive, aggression-based criteria of excellence to supportive, collaborative, interactive ones."[6] It has rediscovered, as well, that true "authority" means "empowering others."[7]

So—better late than never—the emerging church now toys with a shift from vertical style to horizontal style—from rank and status to love and grace—from patron-client roles to Christian brotherhood (believe it or not!). It is a shared journey, a pilgrim companionship, a common walk. It is a non-coercive connectedness, a mutual mentoring, a paradox of following while leading. And no one—including the leader—rises above advice or critique.

It's not so much a top-down structure. It's more like a "solar system" where each planet has its own orbit, its own "gifts." In other words, it's more like a team of "spiritual entrepreneurs" where each believer supports and encourages the other's inspired destiny.

St. Augustine got it right:

> What I am *for* you terrifies me; what I am *with* you consoles me. *For* you I am a bishop; but *with* you I am a Christian. The former is a duty; the latter a grace. The former is a danger; the latter, salvation.[8]

Spinning Off Totally New Riffs

So tomorrow's emerging leaders will build leaders who build leaders.

They will make disciples who make disciples. And, they will equip apostles who equip apostles. Over, and over, and over. . . .

Jesus didn't say, "Go schedule seminars." He said, "Go make disciples."[9] In other words, ministry is done *through* us, not through a conversation *about* us. Through visioning, modeling, mentoring, equipping, risking, and midwifing, the new leaders will empower others to act. They will release the gifts, talents, passions, and energies of all.

That means anyone, anywhere, anytime, and any way. It means incognito missions of every kind—ministries in any walk of life—inspired creativity wherever it's found—entrepreneurship in all Christ-like events. It means both within their community and beyond their community—cross-cultural and counter-cultural—local and global.

This new network is the new notion of "team." It's the paradox of diversity, yet unity—fluid spirit relationships, yet the same Spirit—distinct ways of witnessing, yet the same Word. It's like a jazz ensemble intuitively following the leading of an inspired motive, then creatively responding to variations on that motive. All the while, though, each player supports and encourages the band's unity. Then, suddenly, the band spins off totally new riffs in hot pursuit of the Lord of History.

Getting the Keys to the Car

Does anything go?

As long as the laity are aligned with the mission, they need a long "leash." In other words, they need permission to do their own thing, to feel in control of their own destiny, to dream of more than they've ever dreamed to be. That means removing all the unnecessary barriers, all the things that stifle growth, all the constraints on new ideas.

Such permission, of course, includes permission to make mistakes. Granted, the apparent anarchy and seeming chaos of these mistakes drive perfectionists and control freaks crazy. But risk is a necessary ingredient of creativity, and novices need plenteous room to put their inspiration into play.

Sooner or later, they must be given the keys to the car.

This permission doesn't mean laity have *total* freedom. And it doesn't mean leaders relinquish *total* control. For the leader does not ignore his own anointing or sacrifice his own conviction. And, he's not a pushover or a Casper-milquetoast pastor.

Sometimes, he must step in. He must rescue the participants, hold them accountable, or even throw out the "bad apples." He may allow mistakes, but he doesn't allow mistakes to "take over." He may permit some things, but he doesn't permit *all* things.

Today's emerging leaders confuse permission with permissiveness.

———— ∞∞⦿⦿⦿ ————

Finally, though, transfigured laity mean transfigured leaders. The success of emerging leaders, for example, is no longer the harvest, but the planting—no longer power, but empowerment—no longer personal gifts, but other's gifts.

It's a *different* success.

And, the sculptor Michelangelo knew this difference. Patiently—but passionately—he chipped away the excess marble while allowing God's *own vision* to emerge.

Endnotes

1. John Wesley, quoted in "John Wesley: The Great Methodist," *The Prayer Foundation*, January 1, 2007   http://prayerfoundation

.org/books/book_review_ heroes_john_wesley.htm.

2. See the following random Scriptures: Matthew 23:8-12; Romans 12:3-8; 1 Corinthians 12, 14:26; Ephesians 4:7-16; 1 Thessalonians 5:19-21; James 3:1,2; 1 Peter 4:9-11.

3. 1 Corinthians 14:14-15, 26; Colossians 3:16; Ephesians 5:19.

4. Martin Luther, quoted in "The Living Heritage of Saint Augustine," *Augustine Institute*, January, 2007 http://www.sspxasia.com/Documents/Arch bishop-Lefebvre/Luthers-Mass.htm.

5. Leonard Sweet, *SoulTsunami: Sink or Swim in New Millennium Culture* (Grand Rapids, MI, Zondervan, 1999) p.58.

6. Derrick de Kerckhove, *The Skin of Culture* (Toronto: Somerville House Publishing, 1995) p. 62.

7. Fritjof Capra, *The Hidden Connections: Integrating the Biological, Cognitive, and Social Dimensions of Life into a Science of Sustainability* (New York: Doubleday, 2002) p. 89, 100.

8. St. Augustine, quoted in *Dogmatic Constitution of the Church, Vatican II Council*, http://www.vatican.va/archive/hist_councils/ii_vatican_council/documents/vat-ii_const_19641121_lumengentium_en.html.

9. Matthew 28:18-20.

Who's "In" and Who's "Out"?

But how can laity become leaders if they haven't been to seminary or bible college? How can they share Scripture with integrity if they haven't studied Scripture with integrity? And, how can they expect respect if they haven't been certified for respect?

Or, more to the point, how can "submerged" followers ever deserve to be "emerging" leaders?

After all, our nation was founded on enlightened understanding. The ability to think coherently and systematically was fundamental to "knowing" anything. As a result, our great schools—which began as seminaries!—were prerequisites to serving God "professionally."

But something happened. Academic credentials in the "world of Spirit" lost credibility. They persuaded less because they were believed less. C. S. Lewis put it this way:

> You cannot *study* Pleasure in the moment of nuptial
> embrace, nor repentance while repenting, nor analyze
> the nature of humor while roaring with laughter.[1]

Yet, emerging leaders (especially those who only *study* "religion") assume that everyone outside their "boat" is uninformed and must be informed—that everyone else is out of touch with the philosophical trends and must be filled in—and that everyone not clued in on the facts must be clued in.

They don't realize the world has changed—that there's a different story about who is "in" and who is "out"—that they may be confusing the rescuers with those needing rescuing. They don't realize that we've shifted to an oral culture—that the new spirituality is "unthinkable"—that an emerging world prefers an authentic amateur to a trained professional.

Too many emerging leaders don't realize the world's demand for a new kind of "influence."

Yes, we need wisdom! But true wisdom is more a matter of how to "be" than how to "know." It is an *embedded* knowing, an *incarnate* Truth. For that reason, *life itself makes leaders.* Faith in the midst of failure, sorrow, and crisis forms their essential character. So aspiring leaders need mentoring or "on-the-job training" more than facts or information. And, the quicker spiritual seekers find their ministry the quicker they mature spiritually.

Today's emerging leaders harbor illusions, as well, about who's in charge. Inspiration, obviously, has nothing to do with religious "pecking orders." Whether we're certified or simple, it's the Spirit that's in charge. For example, visions are revealed, not simply created. And, true originality is the privilege of God alone, not simply the product of someone's talent or training.

In other words, we point to Truth *only* out of the Power to which we point.

Whether ordained or ordinary, all of us have known a Power obviously not ours, a quickening from we-know-not-where. We only know that it is a self-authenticating, autonomous force—a *manifest* presence, an *indwelling* reality. For it claims us, shapes us, compels us. . . .

> "To lose ourselves in the performance of an obligation which we accept, in spite of its appearing on reflection impossible of achievement . . . (is) *a clue to God.*"[2]

Uncertified Spiritual Giants

Who are the leaders with wisdom? Those whose lives *confirm* wisdom. Who are the leaders with esteem? Those whose lives *earn* esteem. Who are the leaders with character? Those whose lives *show* character.

Ordinations and degrees—scholarships and schools—politics and positions certainly help. But they're not the true source of spiritual maturity. That's the reason the Lord of History compels the "uncertified" to become spiritual giants—the "unauthorized" to move in incarnate power—the "unentitled" to speak with prophetic boldness.

For "The manifestation of the Spirit is given to *everyone* for profit."[3]

"Everyone" includes the unrefined, the unwashed, the unwanted—the outsiders, the ethnic, the alien—the nobodies, the hopeless, and the least among Christ's brothers and sisters. In fact, history's anointed have most often included people at the margins. Today's India, for example, shows God "working predominantly through women and uneducated people."[4]

More to the point, God does not play second fiddle to any religious edifice, presumption, or pigeonhole. A careful reading of Scripture confirms this. Indeed, this truth proves the very origin of the church.[5]

The more we move into the 21st century, the more we'll look for leaders with depth and character. And we'll find them *anywhere* Spirit takes on body and body takes on Spirit.

In other words, *wherever* the "Word is made flesh."

> "There is, therefore, in Christ and in the Church no inequality . . . 'all these things are the work of one and the same Spirit' . . . (the laity) are in their

own way made sharers in the priestly, prophetical, and kingly functions of Christ."[6]

The *Real* World

Who says spiritual leadership is limited to "religious" leaders? Who says personal ministry is limited to "official" ministries? Who says sacred space is limited to "designated" spaces? And who says sacred time is limited to "announced" times?

Beyond doubt, prophetic voices speak through *any* voice. Caring hearts embolden *any* heart. A manifest Spirit manifests in *any* place. And a move of God moves in *any* time.

In other words, secular work and sacred ministry should fit seamlessly together. The regeneration of Christ overlays our whole reality. We're not compartmentalized! We do what we're led to do—anywhere, anytime.

Even the factory floor becomes a hotbed of creativity or an epicenter of ennobling causes. Every job, of course, begins with applied data and learned skills. But soon it becomes a matter of people, relationships, widening communities, passionate "living," and shared visions.

So what if it's a secular job?

A secular business, after all, may be the best choice for the mission-minded. For successful businesses must respond to global pressures, and their widening influence becomes an open door for compassionate leaders. More important, though, the laity are "where it's at." Their very vocation—the web of their very existence—is where the least, the last, and the lost are found.

> The laity are called in a special way to make the Church present and operative in those places and

circumstances where *only through them* can it
become the salt of the earth . . . (Their ministry) takes
on . . . a special force.[7]

In other words, the laity "work for the sanctification of the world
from within." They "consecrate the world itself to God."[8] Their
world is the *real* world.

Yet, we usually associate ministry with a church "program":
"Remember, work is work, and church is church. So if you're going
to be in ministry, you'd better be in church."

The church says, for example, "Come join *our* conversation," but
history demands, "Join *my* conversation!" The church says, "Be a
volunteer next Sunday," but history insists, "Do something—anywhere—RIGHT NOW!" The church says, "Mission is
among friends *in* the church," but history declares, "Mission is
among strangers *outside* the church."

Our "community," clearly, is far larger than we admit.

Who Was That Masked Man?

On-the-spot ministries in the real world reveal self-evident advantages. Wherever the laity are "on call," they see—first-hand—the
hidden opportunities. And, with personal immediacy, they offer
better solutions and faster results than any religious bureaucrat.

It's a "Spirit of spontaneity." These laity are like football quarter-
backs who call "audibles," or new plays, right on the line of scrim-
mage. Their decisions are proactive, spontaneous responses to facts
on the field.

These let-loose laity also enjoy the advantages of widespread
communities—open systems of networked believers—hubs of
connectivity built around common visions. Their fluid spiritual

partnerships are built around missions, not ministries. And they can accomplish results far larger than the closed systems of any one church or any one denomination can accomplish.

They resemble the far-flung networks of "bloggers" that now outpace even giant news syndicates. In other words, the guys sitting at computers in their pajamas are focusing the flow of world news. Their spheres of influence are living organisms that mobilize the mavericks of creativity and innovation.

Hopefully, emerging church leaders will "get it." They will grasp a real world served by the entrepreneur rather than the religious recluse. They will place a far greater emphasis on the promises of their own unleashed laity.

Surely, that's what Scripture intended. Christians are "sent." They "go out" rather than "come in." They are an "on call" immediacy. Like Philip, in the story of the Ethiopian eunuch,[9] they jump into the "chariot," mentor for a minute, purify the moment, then disappear.

We especially need this "real world ministry" today. For the church has lost considerable influence. In fact, a whole generation has left—only 16% of 18-22 years olds are involved in formalized religion.[10] Freedom *of* religion has turned increasingly toward freedom *from* religion. And there are places where traditional missions—or in-your-face salvations—are flat out forbidden.

Plainly, no one—including the Holy Spirit—likes brute force.

But the laity—freed from formal constraints—can still reach the secular world. And they're already doing it—but not by the "rule book." Their ways can be far more *transparent*. When done in a caring yet hidden way, the world *sees through it* to the Lord. In other words, their message is not a program, a religion, a building, a culture, a doctrine, a system, a style, a club, or a commercial product.

Put another way, their message doesn't have to be "religious" in order to be "religious."

These transparent moments are transformational moments where anything and everything speaks. They are "works of art," where the "arts" are never noticed. They are like watching something catching fire—seeing the familiar turning strange, or seeing the strange turning familiar. More important, though, they are powers that operate outside of organized religion.

For "The wind of the Spirit blows where it wills."[11]

It's All About Courage

None of this is possible if we can't release the laity from the constraints of the typical church. It can't be done, in other words, if we refuse to abandon the stereotypes that have hobbled the laity for so many years. Yes, there are times when the laity should follow. But there are also times when the laity should lead.

The courage in emerging leaders to build courage in emerging laity is an urgently needed bridge to tomorrow's church.

It's all about courage! Assuming today's spiritual leaders have this courage, then the laity need the same courage to let go of the same past. And then—perhaps more important—they need courage to hear their unique calling for the future. After all, they are "both called and empowered to be extensions of the Incarnation"[12]—to become more than they ever thought they could be.

Of course, the laity also need courage to stand alone—unaided, self-directed—yet submitting to the leading of the Spirit. Then, it takes even further courage to "get involved," to participate, to risk vulnerability. And, finally, it takes profound courage to speak prophetically—to speak of "nonexistent things . . . as if they [already] existed"—to give form to the "substance," "evidence" and "proof" of things we do not see.[13]

Such courage presents a strange paradox. It's the courage of *both* humility and risk—selflessness and audacity—submission and trailblazing. It's the courage to hazard God's Power while hastening His Presence. It's the courage, in short, to risk downloading heaven to earth.

> "When they saw the *boldness* . . . of Peter and John . . . they *recognized* that they had been with Jesus."[14]

Networked Entrepreneurs

So the laity are sent out—yet supported. On their own—yet encouraged. And, they rightfully expect this backing.[15] As in a great symphony orchestra, when individual players have a solo, every-one—including the conductor—works in a supportive role, always helping to "empower" the soloist's vision.

That means mentors constantly re-envision the laity's vision. They continuously refire the laity's fires. And, while doing this, they faithfully come alongside in long-term relationships.

Loosening constraints on the laity seemingly leads to a leaderless band of "outlaws." And giving up controls of "everything spiritual" seemingly unleashes uncontrolled chaos. Yet, once emerging leaders get past these fears, their influence will increase, not decrease.

One spiritual leader by himself, for example, can't solve the problems of a million people, but a million people networking together can solve a multitude of problems. This happens when churches morph from organizations into organisms, when the laity shift from volunteers into networked entrepreneurs.

Unloading the Burden

This new relationship with the laity is more than a good idea, more than a good strategy. It is life itself—the very lifeline of the laity—the only true relationship with God. For the correlation of Creator and creation—eternity and history—is the ultimate goal of every sentient being.

Faith, in other words, is not a mere idea—it's not impersonal knowledge "about" God—and it's not the socially acceptable study of religious societies and doctrinal minds. It is not a timeless notion detached from history—it's not a navel-gazing monologue—and it's not a mere toleration of timeless traditions. It is not a second-hand reverie—it's not the passion of proxies—and it's not a vicarious hand-me-down from clerical surrogates.

Faith, instead, is *in-your-face*. It is powerful and personal—spontaneous and transcendent—close and up-front. It is filled with inspirations, insights, felt-meanings, and sudden disclosures. It does not sit on the sidelines. It is totally involved, intimately engaged.

Of course, there are times when faith is passive—simply contemplative.

But, sooner or later, faith is *what-are-you-going-to-do-right-now?* It compels us to participate—challenges us to act—moves us to respond. For we are living manifestations, contingent realities, reciprocal agents. And, we are driven to unload these burdens in the very moments of our history.

This relationship—this new definition of a new laity—is the *only* thing that distinguishes the Judeo-Christian God from every other religion. For our God is the *only* Creator-God, and He created us to create. In other words, we are "coauthors" in a world not so much a "Creation" as a "Creating."

Are You Persuadable?

Change is the price of survival.

The refusal of an empowered laity has proven the greatest failure of today's church. The co-dependency of skeptical pastors—protecting their own financial interests—and lazy laity—protecting their own membership privileges—is an insidious addiction. Unless this cozy collusion stops, other more fervent and faith-filled entrepreneurs will find their own way *outside* the church.

We must re-examine our most deeply held delusions and turn away from our most outdated structures. At the same time, we must responsibly create the emerging guidelines for mentoring and supporting eager entrepreneurs. Yes, structure, education, and resources will always remain a necessity. But they will differ from the past. They will prove, for example, far more flexible and far more "user-friendly."

The Lord of History is releasing the constraints on today's laity. And, it's evident why! The advent of supercomputer intelligence and pagan spirituality will leave lethargic leaders so far behind that Spirit-inspired entrepreneurs will be the only ones left who can walk with empowerment in the real world.

Those who are persuadable—and those who stake out this new frontier—will be the true "emerging leaders" of the 21st century.

> "Let them not, then, hide this hope in
> the depths of their hearts."[16]

Endnotes

1. C. S. Lewis, quoted in Leanne Payne, *Real Presence* (Grand Rapids: Baker Books, 2000) p. 133.

2. Michael Polanyi, *Personal Knowledge: Towards a Post-Critical Philosophy* (Chicago: The University of Chicago Press, 1958) p. 324.

3. 1 Thessalonians 5:12, 19-21.

4. Dr. Victor Choudhrie, a surgeon in Madhya Pradesh, India, quoted in *Friday Fax Newsletter*, 2005, Issue 32, August 19, www.bufton. net/fridayfax

5. A careful reading of the original Greek in Matthew 16:15-18 reveals Jesus founded His church on *spiritual revelation*—not position or personality, intellect or intelligence, education or training.

6. Vatican II Council, *Dogmatic Constitution of the Church*, November 21, 1964 http://www.vatican.va/archive/hist_councils/ ii_vatican_council/documents/vat-ii_const_19641121_lumen-genti um_en.html

7. Vatican II Council.

8. Vatican II Council.

9. Acts 8:29-40.

10. Dick Staub, "An Open Letter to CFC Friends," *CULTURE-WATCH*, March, 2006 http://www.dickstaub.com/culturewatch.php? record_id=987

11. John 3:8 (my paraphrase).

12. C. S. Lewis, pp. 143, 144.

13. Romans 4:17, *New International Version* & *The Amplified Bible*; Isaiah 46:10, *The Amplified Bible*; Hebrews 11:1, *King James Bible* & *The Amplified Bible*.

14. Acts 4:13, *The Amplified Bible*.

15. Vatican II Council.

16. Vatican II Council.

AN ARTIFACT OF SCRIPTURE

Needed but Not Necessary

Among the many things "going out of style," emerging leaders often avoid the traditional role of Scripture. And here's why:

In a world of chaotic uncertainty, we needed a fresh approach to Scripture. And, even before this epic era, we needed a new transparency and a new personal honesty with Scripture. The scriptural "wisdom" of our seminaries, for example, had tended toward "ink on paper, with pages and pages of legal footnotes."[1] And, most academics judged, examined, and argued with the Gospel the way they would a literary artifact.

Outside our schools, the Bible served believers as a mere object of worship or, at best, a moralistic textbook. In other words, it became something spoken *by* us *to* us. Bible-pounding pulpiteers, for example, "knew" the Bible the same way they "knew" the Battle of Gettysburg or their Aunt Jessica's recipe for blackstrap molasses.

But the emerging church "solution"—its "fresh approach"—often signals an alarming indifference toward Scripture. One well-known spokesman calls Scripture a "guideline"—perhaps needed, but not necessary.

Sacred records[2] remind us, though, that our ultimate authority remains the Holy Spirit speaking *through* Scripture—that the "revealed" Word is the *only* Word—that the true "proof text" transcends *both* the interpreter and the interpretation. Scripture, after all, "reads" us more than we read it. It "interprets" us more than we interpret it. And, it "illuminates" us more than we illuminate it—not because it befits a billion rules, but because it's profoundly beautiful!

Scripture has stood the test of time, but it was never time-bound. It owes nothing to either modernity or postmodernity. Whatever the era, it was written—and is written—"with Spirit on spirit."[3]

Endnotes

1. II Corinthians 3:4-6, *The Message Bible*.

2. The Westminster Confession of Faith, as example.

3. II Corinthians 3:4-6, *The Message Bible*.

Private Opinion?

Yet, Scripture has lost much of its voice today. And, it has grown especially silent in the emerging church! Does this mean Scripture has a diminished role in the postmodern world?

For more than two millennia, biblical writers gave form to their inspired revelations. And for two more millennia, we believed in their written inspirations. In short, Scripture proved its own integrity. It was "the norming norm,"[1] the standardizing standard. It was the touchstone, the test—the reliable witness—of Truth.

In other words, it was around long before the distortions of either modernity or postmodernity. For it "is in the hands, but not in the power, of the church."[2] Scripture is Truth, but not necessarily doctrine. It is revealed, but not necessarily "religious."

Unlike man's myopia, Scripture has open-ended power.

It is transcendent, in other words. No Scripture is "a matter of private opinion."[3] No Scripture originated simply "because some man willed it."[4] Indeed, Scripture transcends both the interpreter and the interpreted. It holds the very mystery of our salvation.

Still, it is also transparent. Biblical writers *lived* the events of their revelation. Their stories came from real life, not abstract doctrine or philosophical ideas. Their Truth came through *embodied* Truth, not objective, once-removed reports. In the chaos and mess that follow fallen people in a fallen world, biblical writers offered self-evident signs and self-authenticating tests of Universal Truth.

Yet, sadly, Scripture has been dealt a mortal blow, and the chief culprit—amazingly so!—is modern theology itself.

Ink Stamped on Dead Trees

Good scholarship is a wonderful thing. Yet—in the "spirit" of our time—we have surrendered Scriptural Truth to the "higher" goals of "official systems," "rational structures," and "stored facts." We have relinquished Scriptural revelation to "proposed ideas," "ordained thought," and "intellectual assent."

In other words, scholars "know" Scripture much the way chemists "know" the Periodic Table of Elements.

As a result, Scripture is reduced to a rational structure. Its Word is little more than the syntax of its text. Its Spirit is limited to abstract ideas. And its faith is something that happened in the past. We turn it into a textbook—and then we transform our "academic" truth into an "absolute" truth.

Yet, "absolutes"—by definition—remain independent of even our best scholars. Absolutes, after all, are complete in themselves. So the Truth of Scripture remains free, as well, from our imperfections, from our limitations. Scripture, in other words, stands on its own.

History is exposing the scandalous "proof" of modern theology. And rightly so. For modern theologians reflect the needs of the modern mind more than the intentions of the biblical prophets.

Yet, tragically, Scripture has never recovered from the onslaught of the modern mind.

> "The plan wasn't written out with ink on paper, with pages and pages of legal footnotes, killing your spirit. It's written with Spirit on spirit."[5]
>
> Saint Paul

The Only Word

Scripture, in other words, has no revelation in our Greek "soul," until it is revealed in our Hebrew "spirit." It has no power in our logical mind until it is revealed in our intuitive heart. It's always been that way. Sacred records remind us that the only authority of Scripture is the Holy Spirit speaking *through* Scripture.

After all, there's a difference between *thinking about* Truth and *encountering* Truth. Academic theologians often write and talk about the Holy Spirit, but seldom, it seems, do they *encounter* the Holy Spirit.

Scripture insists that it is "God's Spirit in a person" (the "Spirit of Truth") that "gives men understanding"—that "confirm(s) every-thing" about Jesus—that leads to the "whole, full Truth."[6] Again, Scripture affirms that the *revealed* Word is the *only* Word.

And there's a purpose in this.

Revelation is deeper and wider than the Bible itself. Remember that the Word first entered the world *without* Scripture. In other words, "What (was) born of the Spirit (*was*) spirit."[7] Nothing more, nothing less. The later events of Scripture were surely inspired, but they were, at least, one step removed from the original revelation. As Paul said, "We get what we say straight from God and say it as honestly as we can."[8]

So, in each encounter with Scripture, we're required to reopen its pristine Source. Scripture, after all, is a divinely prepared *medium* of revelation rather than the revelation itself.

This means we must release Scripture from the tyranny of the printed page. Revelation is not ink on paper or mere "words." It is not a linguistic exercise or a literary artifact. It is not what *was taught* or what *was revealed*. It is not a systematic theology or something spoken *by us* to ourselves.

Instead, the revelation of Scripture is ***unwritten***. It is the language of unspokenness. It "is based on not talk but power."[9] It is founded not on "the letter (of legally written code) but of the Spirit."[10] And it has our name written all over it. It is a specific vision for a specific person at a specific time.

It is "reasons of the heart," for which reason knows nothing.[11]

In other words, its pristine insight prints itself first on our spirit. And, in this initial encounter, it depends on a prior-to-words world for its power. It is a different knowing, a deeper knowing. It's a knowing that comes when you've been there, entered in, and experienced firsthand in an unforgettable way. And, though often filled with paradox and enigma, we sympathetically respond.

Only later, with continuing meditative dialogue, do these revelations sometimes turn into "knowledge."

Unlike our knee-jerk analysis, the "Spirit of Truth" brings power to Scripture. First, it hits us personally. It's a self-identity event. It searches us—tests us—challenges us.

And, as we meditate on it—reflect on it—"soak" in it—and "chew" on it, an inspired certainty builds the substructure of our convictions. Indeed, this certainty is the only definitive "proof," the only validating "Voice." For it has a "presence" in our heart—it is just there! Later, it proves itself yet again. For it leads us to a recreated life and an "exclusive" witness of Truth, even as we share an "inclusive" witness of its Authority.

———————— ⟐ ————————

The Lord of history demands a different approach to this ancient, yet futuric, communion with Truth. We must search Scripture as if for the first time. Scholars must finally let Scripture speak on its own.

We must quit robbing Scripture of its open-ended power. In short, we must quit "manipulating" our revelation.

After all, "the world cannot receive . . . the Spirit of Truth," regardless of academic expertise.[12] Yes, the biblical writings on our coffee tables and in our libraries should be revered. But their life-giving power comes only from the quickening of the Holy Spirit.

> "...now breathe your wisdom over me
> so I can understand you."[13]

Endnotes

1. Stanley Grenze and John Franke, quoted in Robert Webber, *The Younger Evangelicals: Facing the Challenges of the New World* (Grand Rapids: Baker Books, 2002) p. 101.

2. Karl Barth, quoted in "Comments on Can We Still Trust God's Word, pt. 3," *Next-Wave*, September 22, 2002 http://www. the-next-wave-ezine.info/issue89/index.cfm?id =12&ref=ARTICLES_FROM%20THE%20ARCHIVES_203

3. II Peter 1:21, *The Message Bible*.

4. II Peter 1:21, *The Amplified Bible*.

5. II Corinthians 3:4-6, *The Message Bible*.

6. Job 32:8, *The Message Bible & The Amplified Bible*; John 15:26, *The Message Bible*; John 14:17 & 16:13, *The Amplified Bible*.

7. John 3:6, *The Amplified Bible*.

8. II Corinthians 2:17, *The Message Bible*.

9. I Corinthians 4:20, *The Amplified Bible*.

10. II Corinthians 3:6, *The Amplified Bible.*

11. Blaise Pascal, quoted in Danielle DuRant, "Blaise Pascal: Reasons of the Heart" *RZIM,* 1997 http://www.rzim.org/resources/jttran. php?seqid=44

12. John 14:17, *The Amplified Bible.*

13. Psalms 119:73, *The Message Bible.*

A POLITICAL BIAS

Trapped in Agenda

The emerging church movement is also plagued by political bias. And its leaders have turned this bias—whether left/right, blue/red, liberal/conservative—into a pseudo-religion, something sacred in itself.

Obviously, every spiritual vision gambles on the future, but most traditional leaders label most emerging leaders as "liberal"—or more to the point, "*too* liberal." Of course, emerging leaders refuse this tag. In the words of one, "We have no politics . . . (we're not) liberals . . . (or) the new Christian Left."[1]

Yet, most observers agree with Shakespeare, "Methinks he protests too much."

Regardless of rampant political bias, there's really no such thing as a "liberal Christian" or a "conservative Christian." Jesus' message, after all, was never a political message. And even today, an older and wiser Billy Graham insists the Gospel plainly "transcends party lines."[2]

Nevertheless, the world views of both liberals and conservatives often offer helpful insights into justified concerns. The tragedy comes when they get trapped—and stay trapped!—in their own agenda.

Liberals, for example, fear form. They fear any spiritual "anchor"—any spiritual accountability, validation, verification. . . . They have no interest, in other words, in bedrock decisions, conclusive judgments, or anything rock-solid "to stand on." For they are *certain about their uncertainty*.

So they are happy with an anything goes, unknowable world. That means they are more interested in freedom than faith—they care more about the medium than the message. It's as if the winners of their debates actually get the privilege of "changing God's mind."

In this same "fear of form," they have become informal and unformed *to an extreme*. And forget about "authority." For they shape their own life, make their own destiny, provide their own authority.

That means they refuse anything that is an affront to their "intelligent" minds. And that refusal includes blind faith, gut-level convictions, and prophetic visions. So—of necessity—they mold all mysteries into politically correct, "user-friendly" ideas.

After all, they're "cool," and they enjoy a "cool" religion.

Conservatives err in other ways. Seldom can we call them, for example, truly "emerging." For they usually defend the church *against* the future. Hidebound, conservative churches are often big, but seldom far-sighted—often influential, but seldom forward looking.

Admittedly, history traces their origins to a true move of God. But somewhere along the way, their leaders started hammering authentic inspiration into doctrine and dogma—chiseling pure revelation into answers for any and every question—constructing elaborate defenses against any and every attack.

With most conservative churches, of course, their original, pristine movement is now over. Spontaneity and innovation is finished. So their leaders continue "mistaking the oyster for the pearl." But if God ever forgets what He is about, they will certainly remind Him!

So *both* political wings of the emerging church have locked themselves within their own realities. But for different reasons. One fears form, the other fears the future. One pushes questions, the other pushes answers. One is certain of its uncertainty, the other is certain of its certainty.

Lethal and immaculate in their own vanities, each side accuses the other of lasting damage to the Gospel. They have polarized their positions. They have become suspicious and defensive—counting those who are "with us" and those who are "against us."

But their wars are self-destructive wars. Incapable of critiquing their own biases, their battles are pathological, even suicidal. Consequently, neither group leads society.

Both have built dams across rivers of pure spirit. Both have failed history.

So, what's the answer? Surely all emerging leaders treasure the memories of their inspired visions. But their report of truth is always several steps removed from their revelation of truth. In other words, rendering the infallible Word is not without error, and living this Word is not without distortion.

That's the human condition.

So a good dose of humility is appropriate for all spiritual leaders—especially when the thin crust of our reality no longer supports the status quo. This imminent collapse is the moment between danger and opportunity, but the honest fear neither correction nor new direction.

This rebirth requires a leap of faith, but few have the spiritual maturity to risk the leap.

In place of hardened dogma or skeptical logic, the faithful allow a benevolent Mystery to break into the present and transform it. In other words, they embrace blind belief prior to bold understandings—they embrace a "wisdom of the heart" prior to the intelligence of the mind—and they embrace aesthetic Truth prior to conceptual truth.

For their inspiration has only begun its long journey toward insight.

Sooner or later, though, they must make sense of their senses—they must understand their understandings. The Spirit must take on body, and the body must take on Spirit. So they give "substance," "evidence," and "proof" to things previously unknown.[3]

And what a relief it is to return to the secure sanity of grounded knowing.

. . . but they can't stay there long. Their "knowing" is a cycle of grace, an ongoing rhythm of repentance—revelation—and interpretation. . . . In this perpetual dialogue, they weave in and out of having answers and not having answers. Because God's world is not so much a "Creation" as a "Creating."

> "All of us . . . are constantly being transfigured into
> His very own image in ever increasing splendor and
> from one degree of glory to another."[4]

Endnotes

1. Anonymous, to protect an emerging leader.

2. Billy Graham, quoted in Jon Meacham, "Pilgrim's Progress" *Newsweek*, August 14, 2006, p. 41.

3. Hebrews 11:1.

4. II Corinthians 3:18, *The Amplified Bible*.

Are You Winning the Cultural War?

W e live in an extraordinary time. Future historians will split this
era into "before" and "after." Our "endings" and "beginnings"
used to be incremental, now they're exponential. And in their
headlong rush, history forces goodbyes to all the things already gone
by.

Nothing has "gone by" more than the clash between Christian
"conservatives" and "liberals." The current news regarding their
cultural war is irrelevant—one of the illusions of our time. And here
is why:

Though each group fervently believes the other has "missed
it"—though each group believes they are history's "chosen
ones"—though each group plots the destruction of the other ("in the
name of love and compassion," of course), *both groups have been
firmly rejected by the postmodern world.*

The unchurched masses, for example, are not impressed by "hypoc-
risy in religious poses." They are not moved by "money and power
in pious garbs." And they are not affected by "empty pieties within
worn-out traditions." Their disinterest has turned menacingly toward
even a dislike of the church. The more rebellious ones, for example,
insist that "faith in God is not only out of date, but (even) dangerous."[1]

No wonder Christianity is now called a "subculture."[2] No wonder it
looks more and more like an old "pink Cadillac with huge tail fins."[3]
And, no wonder rock groups sing, "Theologians don't know nothing
about my soul."[4]

And the upshot of these disaffections? . . .

We live in an age of theological anarchy—a virtual vacuum of *any* truth.

"The Emperor Wears No Clothes"

Certainly, both conservatives and liberals rightly celebrate their previous destinies. Liberals, for example, expanded civilization with universal rights in opposition to slavery, democracy in rejection of monarchy, freedom of the individual in place of herd mentality, and investigative science in resistance to superstition.

Surely, we are grateful!

Yet, the harm liberals have done now outweighs the good. For finally, they have *reduced* life—not expanded it. Their doctrinal formulas, restricted definitions, rigged rhetoric, and narrow science demand claim to "*all* truth." Yet, even their most "profound" revelations remain "in-house"—mere agreements among themselves.

So, in their world of pigeonholed priorities, narrow analysis proceeds from the narrow analyst. In their world of fragmented expertise, "people in similar but specialized fields . . . find it hard to communicate."[5] And, in their Tower of Babel disciplines, truth gets shattered into countless pieces—partial truths, narrow truths, shallow truths—seldom encompassing truths.

It's no surprise, then, these modern sages also restrict themselves more to "thinking" than "doing"—inaction than action, contemplation than improvisation, teaching than modeling, labeling than experiencing. . . .

Yet, their "thinking" remains law! Their politically correct "thought-police" allow only "acceptable" worldviews and disallow "unacceptable" worldviews. Though liberals profess "freedom for all," their coldly closed ideas and harsh intolerance demand the very conventions that rob others of their freedom:

It is impossible, this much is clear, to exaggerate the
heroic self-inflation of academic literary and cultural
criticism.[6]

Of course, the church hasn't escaped their criticism. The modern
world—with its philosophy of liberalism—came into existence as an
"anti-religion" movement. The "Enlightenment," we should
remember, stood brutally against all nonrational—even
transrational—claims. Again, "One enormously precious baby was
tossed with tons of unpleasant bathwater."[7]

Ever since, liberals have remained suspicious of "transrational"
(beyond-the-logic-of-the-mind) religion. Many, in fact, reject *any*
religion. As a result, much of the liberal movement abandoned its
interior life—its transrational or spiritual life—to the conservatives.
Liberal churches, of course, sincerely embrace their own gospel. Yet,
that gospel often reduces "the huge mysteries of God to the respect-
ability of club rules."[8]

Assuming that God is bigger than we say He is—that His manifest
power and presence are more than myth—that our own leading role
with the Lord of History is more than poetry—then the liberal attack
on conservatives seems pathological, even suicidal. For the more
they succeed in destroying the conservatives, the more they destroy
themselves.

Yes, liberals are still in charge of our schools and our liberal politics,
and they remain the planet's dominant force (though relatively few
in number). But their game is up. History has rejected liberalism.
The world now challenges its . . .

> . . . internal self-contradictions, its failed political
> agenda, the harsh intolerance of the politically correct
> thought-police, its claim to be superior in a world
> where nothing is supposed to be superior . . . (In

short, liberalism has) spectacularly failed the test.[9]

Like the old fairy tale, this emperor "wears no clothes."

A Box Within a Box Within a Box

What about conservatives? After all, 70 percent of the world's population is conservative.[10] And, in a way, that's good. When liberals abandoned "interior" faith in preference for "exterior" facts—when they turned away from "vertical" dialogue to "horizontal" debate—somebody had to protect society from the anarchy of the mind.

This protection, this preservation, has always proven the "backbone" of society—the substructure, the cohesion, the unifying factor. It represents, after all, our collective memory, the history of our experience, the proven benefits of our knowing, the "time capsule" of our glory.

It has always been the "destiny" of the conservative church.

Yet—like liberalism—we've been harmed by this great tradition. All the protection and preservation in the world can't make up for the misuse of tradition. Conservatism easily sets up a chain of events where we gradually credit the power of God to doctrine itself. In other words, we slowly imprison ourselves within our own realities.

No doctrine escapes the soiled hands of man's interpretation. So questionable doctrines are always backed up by questionable decrees. And questionable decrees are always propped up by "grim and meaningless" clichés:[11]

> The uncritical use of tradition . . . is essentially an
> archaic or dogmatic traditionalism that is determined
> simply by rigid formulas and ingroup prejudices.[12]

Still, doctrine—good or bad—"must be protected." So, we must fortify it against all threats. And those threats include any revelation larger than our understanding of it—any creativity cut loose from "acceptable" moorings—and any prophetic voice challenging existing "realities."

Such "protection," of course, creates closed minds. And closed minds invite ignorance.

Ignorance, then, easily opens to the manipulation of others: Prepackaged evangelism with cookie-cutter salvations win more souls by man than by God's Spirit. Of course, the goal is quantity, not quality. And these souls are won more by fear than by joy, more by sin than by grace. Manipulating clergy are, in reality, life insurance salesmen, promoting their benefits package.

Conservatives, with their uncritical traditions, have missed both the intentions of the first century and the interests of the twenty-first century. Hidebound, doctrinal rulers can't hear as deeply as God speaks. They can't move as quickly as God moves. And they can't repent as rapidly as God demands.

The credibility of the conservative church has been lost somewhere in a box within a box within a box. . . .

"So Yesterday"

Am I being unfair to either conservatives or liberals? Have I overstated the case? Should I even apologize?

After all, everyone reports revelation in his or her own way. And, whatever the revelation, it reveals a portion of truth—and that truth should be honored. Further, there will always be conservatives and liberals. More important, they will always "perform crucial functions . . . they are the necessary foundation stones for further development."[13]

Yet, something is wrong.

Current history refuses both traditions. Conservatism and liberalism may be the "foundation stones," but they are *not* the "further development." The tools that achieved results in our era are *not* attaining results in the next era. The "progress" and "improvements" of modern culture have *not* found a path into postmodern culture.

Why?

In rare moments, history outstrips our understanding, and the past becomes almost useless as a compass for the future. Today, for example, we confront "a pervasive and often painful uncertainty about how hearing God's voice actually works."[14]

So, in this vacuum of paradigms we invent paradigms—postmodernism, the "cultural creatives," "evolutionary psychology," and on and on—all of which have failed in their vision for our time. Of course, "newly awakened" emerging leaders usually choose postmodernism for their "poster boy." But the narcissism of postmodernists—"You do your thing, I'll do mine"—has proven a great destroyer of Truth. Truth, after all, places an unwelcome demand on them, so they must strenuously "deconstruct" it.

And don't forget, "Nobody tells us what to do."

A Compromised "Legitimacy"

Yet, in humility, what should we do?

We should begin by seeing the "big picture." If we can see where we are and see its risks, we've already solved most of our problems.

Seeing the "big picture" includes seeing this: "Religion is not identical with spirituality; rather religion is the form spirituality takes in civilization."[15] In other words, "The chief role of religion is that of legitimating the socially constructed world."[16] And, in the end, we always compromise that "legitimacy."

Here's an example:

Most would say a successful culture simply needs more love and compassion. But lots of "love and compassion" was the very problem of the Nazis. The Nazis loved their God, their families, their race, their culture. Yet, their "love" led to unbelievable death and destruction. Need we be reminded that "religion" has waged more war than any other pretense in history?

So we must finally recognize the fallibility of every tradition. We must finally recognize that man's truth is only partial truth. And, yes, each must recognize his or her own fallibility, as well. Few Christians, for example, can consistently discern the difference between "flesh" and "spirit." For the fantasies of our religion

> make (us) feel good because they are in harmony with
> (our) opinions, prejudices, and unconscious assump-
> tions about the nature of reality.[17]

Again, I call on emerging church leaders to avoid using tricks, formulas, and gimmickry—to avoid mimicking the distortions and inventions of culture—to avoid confusing intellectual sophistication or the hierarchical positions of power and prestige with mature spirituality. . . .

. . . for the thin crust of our reality is too weak to support the status quo.

———————— ••ə•●●ə•• ————————

Of course, emerging leaders also need a good dose of humility. Both conservatives and liberals need to reconsider the notion that their doctrines, rituals, symbols, styles, ideas, or philosophies are the *only* mediators to God's Presence. And, both conservatives and liberals need to relax their grip on narrow and shallow zealotry.

Like Ezekiel, who was driven into exile, yet knew God's presence in a strange land, emerging church leaders have also become a religious remnant and must seek God's presence in an equally "strange land." And, like Ezekiel's followers, who later returned from exile, yet knew no identity as a national cult, we, too, must create new communities that transcend their identity with contemporary cults.

After all, we're being *reintroduced* to God.

Endnotes

1. R. Albert Mohler, Jr., "The End of Faith—Secularism with the Gloves Off," *The Christian Post,* August 19, 2004 http://www. christianpost.com/article/20040819/6130.htm

2. Mark Driscoll, quoted in Sarah Means, "Postmodern church targets Generation X in Seattle," *Thunderstruck*, August 12, 1998 http://www.thunderstruck.org/holysmoke/marshill.htm

3. Leonard Sweet, *Post-modern Pilgrims: First Century Passion for the 21st Century World* (Nashville, TN: Broadman & Holman: 2000) p.2.

4. Dick Staub, "Theologians Don't Know Nothing,"*Culture Watch*, September 3, 2004 http://dickstaub.com/culturewatch.php?record_ id=737

5. Joseph D'Agnese, "Scientific Method Man" *WIRED* 09/2004 pp.112-121.

6. Frank Lentricchia, quoted in Ken Wilber, *A Theory of Everything: An Integral Vision for Business, Politics, Science, and Spirituality* (Boston: Shambhala, 2000) p. 4.

7. Ken Wilber, *A Theory of Everything: An Integral Vision for Business, Politics, Science, and Spirituality* (Boston: Shambhala, 2000) p. 81, 82.

8. Eugene H. Peterson, *The Message//Remix: The Bible in Contemporary Language* (Colorado Springs: NavPress, 2003) p. 1860.

9. Wilber, pp. 79, 80, 124, 125.

10. Wilber, p. 134.

11. C. S. Lewis, quoted in "The 'Authentic' C. S. Lewis" *Culturewatch*, May 28, 2004 http://dickstaub.com/culturewatch.php?record_id=686

12. Thomas C. Oden, *Systematic Theology: The Living God* (San Francisco: Harper & Row, 1987), p. 338.

13. Wilber, p. 118.

14. Dallas Willard, *Hearing God: Developing a Conversational Relationship with God* (Downers Grove, Illinois: InterVarsity Press, 1999) p. 25.

15. William Irwin Thompson, *The Time Falling Bodies Take to Light: Mythology, Sexuality, and the Origins of Culture* (New York: St. Martin's Press, 1981) p. 103.

16. Grenz and Franke, *Beyond Foundationalism: Shaping Theology In A Postmodern Context* (Louisville: Westminster John Knox Press, 2001) p. 76.

17. Thompson, p. 92.

A POPULAR "SPIRIT"

The Latest "Buzz"

Whether liberal or conservative, emerging leaders believe they must prove they are up-to-date. So they seek an accommodation to the spirit of the *present* world. They feel compelled to make Christianity more "relevant" to spirit of *this* age. They beat their drums for a new theology "by, for, and about" the spirit of *today's* generation.

Their ultimate illusion, in other words, adapts God to "where people are at."

So the emerging church finds its legitimacy in the latest "buzz." This legitimacy includes researching the "market," then bringing commercial success to their "product." It includes Madison Avenue marketing and show-business spirituality. And it includes *anything that sells*—even the hidden (or not so hidden) seductions of sex.

Of course, kids are the main targets. With the latest lingo and state-of-the-art technology, emerging leaders morph the "cool" of kids into a religion.

Why not? We're all creatures of culture. We all need a sense of belonging. We all seek sympathetic agreement with how the world works. So it's no big surprise that we've always tailored religion to the tastes of culture. We've always made "religion" a socially acceptable agreement about who God is. And, whenever necessary, we've always reinvented faith to conform to that vision.

And how do we get away with it? We simply "baptize" culture.

The resulting problems should be obvious. Culture is not the same as Spirit. Never was, never will be. In fact, it's hard to imagine a worse fit. Cloaking Spirit with culture leads only to consensual delusions, for we end up being something *other than* who we think we are—or even *the opposite of* who we think we are. This is a dangerous game we're playing, for any belief contrary to the original message is—by definition—"heresy."

Yet, wait. Shouldn't the church want to be effective in its community and in its culture? Shouldn't the church want to connect successfully with anyone and everyone—anytime and anywhere? And shouldn't the church want to "talk the talk," to find relevance in "real" life, to speak the language of the "latest" and the "greatest". . . .

. . . especially when a new culture is "emerging"—and, even more especially, when the Lord of History is "moving"?

Yes, but we do these things blindly. Usually, the latest medium becomes the latest "Message," the latest trend becomes the latest "Word," and the latest ethos becomes the latest "Spirit." In this caricature of culture, counterfeit "signs" move deceptively close to the real—illusory "angels of light" hide deceitfully from our discernment—and bogus "spiritualities" masquerade cunningly as spiritual "kicks."

So it seems we're "damned if we do and damned if we don't." Where are we missing it?

To begin, too many emerging leaders put too much trust in anything "new." They track the "cutting edge" *at any cost*. They think, "If we can just get 'far out' enough, God will be there." But this reflects the unfortunate confusion between "keeping relevant" and "keeping up"—or between "relevancy" and "recency."[1]

After all, something new can become an overnight cliché just as easily as something old. In other words, the most "relevant" is not necessarily the most "recent." A suicide leap into the "unknown"—without a powerful hold on the "known"—does not open up new worlds. There's a difference, after all, between "trends" and "transcendence."

Yet, to accept the message of the emerging church is to accept culture. And to accept culture is to accept the message of the emerging church. That means secular spirituality—whether unreal or surreal, wild or otherwordly—remains "untested, undiscerned, and ungrounded."[2]

Such foolishness flies in the face of the Gospel which is totally autonomous to culture—completely unconstrained by culture. For the Good News is transpersonal, transcultural, and transrational.

Yes, the Lord of History is "always doing something new." But His "newness" is not a trendy "newness." His Truth, for example, is not a matter of something in style or out of style. Instead, it's a matter of something hidden in a live metaphor or lost in a worn-out metaphor—old or new. Transcendence, in other words, comes only from the tension between the unknown and the known—the tension, for example, between "being in tune with the Spirit" and "being in touch with culture."[3]

More than "infinite passion" for our culture, we need "passion for the infinite." Again, culture can't hear as deeply as God speaks. It can't move as quickly as God moves. And, it can't repent as rapidly as God demands.

The emerging church risks the re-emergence of a pagan culture. And, emerging leaders won't be able to criticize culture if they've already become culture.

Endnotes

1. Leonard Sweet, quoted in Peter Walker and Tyler Clark, "Missing the Point?" *Relevant Magazine*, Issue 21, July-August, 2006, pp 70-74.

2. Gordon D. Fee, *Paul, the Spirit, and the People of God* (Peabody, Massachusetts: Hendrickson Publishers, 1996) p. 188.

3. Sweet.

A Musical Example

How do we discern *His* transcendence within *our* culture? How do we find spiritual "relevance" within a trendy "recency"? How do we keep "in tune with the Spirit" while keeping "in touch with a popular 'spirit'"? How do we know if we're going with God or grieving God?

I'll illustrate with the arts—specifically, the art of music. Sensitive spirits often ask, for example, "What makes music—separate from the text or title—Christian?"

Our understanding begins with Hosea. In the original Hebrew, Hosea explains that God speaks to us through *damah*, meaning "prophetic metaphor."[1] Astonishingly, it was also the "art" of the ancient Hebrews. It was—and remains—a perfect model of art. If we understand the laws of *damah* we finally understand the laws of all the arts. We finally understand the awesome power of transcendent worship. And we begin to understand the changing language of a changing world.

Scriptural *damah* demands the dramatic tension between the "known" and the "unknown":

The "known" is anything familiar, friendly, relevant—anything that points to our own identity or the group's identity. It's a common language (artistic or literal). It is reality as we know it—our way of thinking, our established notions, our traditions. In short, the "known" is whatever is safe, comfortable, routine, run-of-the-mill, or ordinary.

The "unknown," on the other hand, is anything unrelated to the known—anything that contradicts or conflicts with the known. By comparison with the known, the "unknown" is absurd, filled with nonsense, and often it becomes a play or parody on the known. It is usually obscure, subtle, hidden, enigmatic, paradoxical, or mysterious. In short, it is anything beyond what we expect—anything beyond the normal—anything that boldly intrudes into our comfortable world.

We find, then, Hosea's *damah*—the tension between the "known" and the "unknown"—*anytime, anywhere, and anyway* "the Word is made flesh."

Back, now, to our musical example:

Music reveals endless tensions between the "known" and "unknown." A good rhythm, for example, requires both the "known" beat and the risk of unusual or even contradicting rhythms (the "unknown"). A good melody requires both the "known" melodic "idea" and the variations or enigmas to that idea (the "unknown"). A good harmony hovers around its tonal center yet always morphs into unrelated (or "unknown") sonorities before finally resolving into its "known" center.

Tone colors paint also with metaphoric timbres. Though rarely found among bland bands of contemporary worship, contrasting (or "unknown") textures, instruments, and chord structures offer refreshing relief to the drone of the "expected"—the tedium of the "known."

Form, too, offers the necessary contrast between the "known" and the "unknown." A simple ABA song structure—with the contrasting middle section—serves our example. But we find an even "deeper" form that also brings us face-to-face to the "Word."

First, some background. . . .

In every century—every culture—Christian liturgy stands on *three moods*: (1) struggle, (2) assurance, and (3) celebration. These moods—with or without the words!—rehearse the Christian story in its most basic form: (1) There is darkness in the world, (2) Jesus came to bring light, and (3) He triumphed over the darkness. Music conveying that story—that "Word"—stands on the same three moods, combined dramatically either within the music or with things external to the music.

In other words, it's the *enigmatic combination* of these "known" moods—struggle, assurance, and celebration—that conveys the Christian experience—the Christian message. Or, we could say it is the "unknown" *paradox* of differing or even opposing moods that creates an inner tension and moves us toward the "Word."

Seldom do we find all three moods—especially with dramatic tension—in today's church music. One mood at a time is the dull order of the day:

Other than angry Gen-X bands, church musicians rarely perform the mood of "struggle" intentionally. But we often experience unintentional struggle through poor electronic reinforcement, poor acoustics, poor rehearsal, or poor performance. Obviously, the mood of struggle—by itself—self-destructs.

A more typical mood in our carpeted sanctuaries is the wall-to-wall sound of "assurance." We also run elevators and dairy farms with it. Yet, this mood carries a deceptive danger! When music endlessly glosses over the cross with saccharine prettiness and syrupy comfort, it costs listeners nothing! It's an easy reverie—a cheap illusion—a passive inaction. Without life-changing resolve, listeners simply refuse their promise. And God warns, "Because you are lukewarm and neither cold nor hot, I will spew you out of My mouth!"[2]

Many churches, though, live in a continual mood of "celebration." "If we can just get everybody dancing and shouting, we've had 'church'." Not so, if we have forgotten what we are celebrating—what we have overcome. Too often, we enjoy the trip without gratitude for the journey. Our make-believe ecstasy proves only natural glee. So in place of true spiritual victory, we indulge only a catchy, bouncy, jolly, earth-stomping, toe-tapping swing. It's a hollow hilarity—a cheap ecstasy. It's as empty as the bubbles in Lawrence Welk's bubble machine.

Instead, Christian "celebration" should always look over its shoulder. Our resurrection should always remember its cross. Otherwise (to paraphrase Isaiah) "Woe unto those" who turn themselves on, but "do not regard the deeds of the Lord."[3]

So when music speaks with *damah*—with prophetic metaphor—with the tension between the "known" and the "unknown"—with the nonsensical stretch between differing or even opposing moods, we begin to do what God called us to do.

But not without risk. . . .

The wonder, suspense, and expectancy in music require risk, surrender, and sacrifice. These are the risks of faith. Without risk, music will remain like a squirrel in a squirrel cage—endlessly retracing the same steps, but going nowhere. Yet with risk, each performance, each song, will bring a totally new revelation. And it will surprise the performers as much as the listeners.

Only then can we say, "Our music is Christian." Only then can we keep "in tune with the Spirit" while—at the same time!—keeping "in touch with the popular 'spirit'."

Surely, we were meant to reach people "where they're at." But whether in church or out of church, sacred or secular, in style or out of style, art or artless, the Word must be transcendent. . . .

. . . that means it must also be *transparent*. . . .

Endnotes

1. Hosea 12:10.

2. Revelation 3:16, *The Amplified Bible.*

3. Isaiah 5:11, 12; *The Amplified Bible.*

PART TWO

HIDDEN OPPORTUNITIES

A NEW TRANSPARENCY

"Yes, Virginia, there is a 'Silver Bullet'"

How much transformation is it going to take? How can the emerging church get past all the traps of culture—the philosophical fads, the political correctness, the consensual delusions? How can it get past the caricatured excess of our spiritual immaturity? And how can it get past the suicide pacts of in-your-face offenses and defenses.

In short, how can we prevent the collapse of the emerging church movement?

Thank God for a "silver bullet." And we find it in one word: "transparency." *The emerging church must rediscover its transparency.*

Transparency comes when everything we do points beyond itself—when all events surpass their appearance—when we see right through to something profoundly pristine and pure. Our every action, in other words, becomes transcendent, transpersonal, transcultural, transrational, *trans-everything*. . . .

We become clean slates where events write on us rather than our writing on events. For only then is our faith enlarged—only then do we see a "bigger picture"—and only then do we share a more generous orthodoxy.

Transparency is neither territorial nor turned-in—neither stagnant nor static—neither objective nor subjective. "(It) does not come with signs to be observed or with visible display, Nor will people say, Look! Here [it is]! or, See, [it is] there!"[1]

It is free of external circumstances.

Why should we ignore transparency? Why should we be an obstacle to the church? Why should we offend unnecessarily? At such a wrenching moment, why should we increase the pain? There's a difference, after all, between premeditated love and premeditated murder—between holy martyrdom and meaningless suicide—between spiritual maturity and spiritual rebellion.

Even the wildest biblical prophets moved in the transparency of their prophecies.

Why can't we do as well?

Endnote

1. Luke 17:20, EXP; Luke 17:21, *The Amplified Bible.*

Rediscovering Transparency

Transparent leadership has always required transparent language. Today especially! For a new language is demanding new ways of saying what we say—meaning what we mean—and signifying what's significant. Or—put another way—a new language tran- scends our tunnel vision self-interests—sidesteps our knee-jerk environment—and rises above our "well-intentioned efforts . . . to 'get it all together' for God."[1]

In short, this new language will get beyond the god-awful shadows that follow the accident-prone "lovers of the literal."

This language will no longer describe "what is." Instead, it will describe "what is coming to be!" It will no longer "supervene" in life—that is, merely "add to life." Instead, it will "intervene" in life—it will actually "change" life.

Few emerging leaders have explored this new language, and still fewer claim any fluency in it.

Surprisingly, the language of the future was also the language of the ancient past. We've simply lost it! As we shared earlier, Hosea confirms that God speaks to us through *damah*—or "prophetic metaphor." That's the reason inspired prophets were creators of comparison and contrast—artists of analogy and affinity—virtuosos of similarity and similitude. . . .

And that's the reason Jesus announced His transcendent truth through transparent metaphor. It's also the reason Jesus, Himself, was the greatest metaphor of all time. This God/man said, "Anyone who has seen Me has seen the Father."[2] His ministry, in other words, was transparent! We see now why both Scripture and ancient history embraced prophetic metaphor as the very language of God!

Today, once again, *damah* is transcending all the failed language of the past. For we are returning to the prophetic metaphor of an oral culture—or, in our case, an "electronic" oral culture. The oral tradition of the ancient Hebrews—where sensory images point out of the power to which they point—"is still the most powerful code . . . and will remain the principal one for the foreseeable future."[3]

And, once again, prophetic metaphor also transcends all studies of meaning. For we are returning to the wisdom of *damah*—only this time, it's a "virtual reality" *damah*. Though not reality itself, Virtual Reality is becoming the most profound medium of reality. Its fiction is proving more powerful than "fact," and its vision is proving more factual than "fiction."

In the words of biblical mystics, it will speak "of nonexistent things . . . as if they [already] existed." It will declare "the end and the result from the beginning."[4] Or, in the words of a modern mystic, Virtual Reality will prove "the most fertile power possessed by man."[5]

So emerging leaders must learn to speak this new language. That means putting things side by side that don't go together, holding the tension between the known and the unknown—the prudent and the prophetic—the predictable and the unpredictable—the credible and the incredible. . . .

In fact, the spiritual linguists of the future must become "virtual" themselves! They must become "conservative daredevils" and "cautious prophets"—speaking with "concise ambiguity". . . .

. . . and "*vivid transparency*."

Endnotes

1. Eugene H. Peterson, *The Message//Remix: The Bible in Contemporary Language* (Colorado Springs: NavPress, 2003) p.

2183.

2. John 14:9, *The Amplified Bible.*

3. Derrick de Kerckhove, *The Skin of Culture* (Toronto: Somerville House Publishing, 1995) p. 193.

4. Romans 4:17, Isaiah 46:10; *The Amplified Bible.*

5. José Ortega y Gasset (in his description of metaphor).

Virtual Reality

C an you speak the language of the future?

Already tomorrow's "words" move too fast to guarantee their meaning out of a much slower past. Already new stories emerge in forms totally unknown by earlier norms. Already digital thoughts fly terribly apace beyond known time and space.

And technology propels this new language at an exponentially quickening pace. The Internet, for example, is much more than a medium. It's the biggest system the world has ever seen, and it grows with incredible speed. In the same way, Virtual Reality is more than virtual. It has captured the popular imagination before reaching anything close to maturity, and it will soon take over the economy as television did.[1]

More important, *Virtual Reality will become the language of the future*. Whether we surf the Net or not, everyday language will respond to the overtones of this fundamental reality. If in doubt, check out the youth. Increasingly, they are the ones who intuitively know the future and who confidently make the technology decisions in their households.

This digital divide stands between even younger and older teens. One study revealed 13-year-olds already more advanced in tech-- savvy language than 16-year-olds.[2]

Of course, no language springs into full-blown existence. So, the gestation between "then" and "not-yet" breeds vital experi- ments—strange bedfellows—and open-ended change.

It's a crazy, creative destruction.

Sometimes more destructive than creative. With the collapse of the modern world, this new language outruns our reality—outpaces our theology. If we survive, we must speak a new speech and sing a "new song."

A New "Language" of Language

The fact that we lack a name for this language proves its newness. It is not another language in the usual sense—mere sounds, sentences, and lexicons. It's more like an emerging language within a language—or what happens when the "language" of *language itself* transforms.

It's safe to say this new language will share understanding more than simply exchange information. It will create worlds more than just observe worlds. It will spring from organic sources more than it will build on mere ideas.

And, cross-cultural in style, it will appeal to the universals of relational experience and real-life emotion. In its finest form, it could be called the "language of beauty," for it will achieve an essential aesthetic presence. And, in this presence, it will become a revelational language—a metaphoric language—a spiritual language, for whatever "is born of the Spirit *is* spirit."[3] And within the pregnant silence of this Otherness, it will also become the language of unspokenness—for "The Kingdom of God . . . is based on *not* talk but power."[4]

In short, this new language will mark a shift from logic to revelation, from mind to spirit, from proposition to the intuition, from the literate to the prophetic. . . .

A New Interface

Technology has a lot to do with this shift. The demands of interactive games, computer dialogue, and the chaos of innovation have spawned endless incompatible systems. Even cyberspace itself creates an incompatible boundary between the real world and an invisible world beyond our grasp.

Something, somehow, had to bridge the gap—had to break the boundaries—had to communicate between separate systems. That something was "interface design." It began with nothing more than a picture of a trash can on the desktop (or the main display screen) of a computer where we could throw away things just like at a real desk.

Gradually, however, this "interface" became a new art that hovered over meaningful silences between seemingly incongruous systems. And the hidden inflections, innuendos, and suggestions inherent in this new language became the "Virtual Reality"—the dialogue—the language of the future.

But we can't understand the language of the future until we realize that *the power in Virtual Reality is a metaphoric power*. Whether eternal images frozen in time or living narratives moving in time, the future belongs to those who can create and communicate prophetic metaphor.

We commonly call metaphors mere "colors" in writing, "figures" in speech, "ornaments" in language. These are only "literary" metaphors, of course. Our very lives move, instead, with another metaphor—a more profound metaphor that violates logic and learning. We easily compare, for example, a sound to a smell, or a sight to a touch—crossing endless modes of expression—creating awesome similarities of the unsimilar.

And, we commonly call Virtual Reality only "virtual"—not really real. Of course, every art form, ritual, symbol, or metaphor is "virtual." And, in all of them, their hidden feelings represent something "not there"—something beyond themselves, something not seen. Yet, like faith, they give "substance" to their vision.[5] More important, they have the power, through God's grace, to transform us—to recreate us—even to heal us.

Why? Because they speak an *incarnational language*—a language that points out of the power to which it points. If we lose this metaphoric power, we have lost Truth Itself. That's the reason Jesus spoke in parables. We often reject transcendent ideas when the message is too great or the gap too wide between our minds and a greater reality. But *prophetic metaphor* bypasses the natural mind and speaks directly to the heart.

———— ⚜ ————

Increasingly, fiction is no longer fiction. Virtual Reality is no longer virtual. The new interface of cyberspace and the "reality" it spawns is birthing the language of the future—a language of immediate experience and felt meanings—a language of mosaics, multiples, and metaphors—a language of amazing and pervasive art—a language of new signs and tests of ancient Truth. . . .

. . . a language of both "online" and "offline" worlds—a language of new realities and new lives!

Endnotes

1. Derrick de Kerckhove,*The Skin of Culture* (Toronto: Somerville House Publishing, 1995) p. 93.

2. Forrester Research, quoted in "Techie Teens," *PC Magazine*, August 2001, p. 30.

3. John 3:6; *The Amplified Bible*.

4. I Corinthians 4:20, *The Amplified Bible*.

5. Hebrews 11:1.

Prophetic Metaphor

When things are rich in ambiguity, enigma, and paradox, know that metaphor is nearby. When things are compared—without common sense—to other things, know that metaphor lurks about. When the revelation of the "real" comes from things *not* real, know that metaphor hides in disguise.

When the known and the unknown combine in impossible ways, know that a certain resonance bounces off things we can't see. When strange tensions between opposing forces crack our credibility, know that these tensions birth hidden Truths. When simple metaphors pile on top of each other in fathomless complexity, know that the invisible is becoming visible.

These tensions resemble a violin string that produces a meaningful melody *because* it is fastened hard at opposite ends. Or, it is like the archer's bow that propels its intentional arrow *because* of the tautness between the bow's opposing poles.

We've known these contradictions. We've felt, for example, the secret grief of the happy clown. We've sensed Negro spirituals that sing of joy and sorrow at the same time. We've tasted, simultaneously, sweetness and sacrifice at a daughter's wedding. And, we've heard about the tragic cross and the triumphant grave in the same moment.

In such moments, unbearable ugliness is not without the atonement of overpowering beauty. And worldly tragedy is not without otherworldly triumph.

But not all metaphors serve Truth. With some metaphors, truth is not even an issue!

Simple metaphors, everyday conventions, or common ideas—like a "warm" welcome, a "big" day, or a "close" friend—have long lost their metaphoric power. And, we seldom find truth in the metaphors of a passing culture where novelty, fad, style, taste, and decor are quickly consumed and soon forgotten. Nor will we find signs of Truth in the metaphors of skilled inventions—the colorful idioms, rhetorical flourish, and figures of speech of our fleshly cleverness.

So we must challenge the difference between surface metaphor and prophetic metaphor—"dead" metaphor and "live" metaphor—a tool of trade and a talisman of transcendence.

"The Whole Fabric"

We have little choice in the matter.

Our culture harbors the mistaken notion that metaphor belongs only to poets. But few realize we actually *exist* in metaphor! Science has discovered, for example, "that most human thought is metaphorical."[1] It is one of the most powerful influences in our daily lives. It plays an enormous role in shaping our understanding of daily events.[2]

Though good writers also invent their "literal" metaphors, metaphor—in its everyday form—remains integral to all language. A handful of basic metaphors, for example, underlies tens of thousands of words in every language.[3] Indeed, metaphor is indispensable to our understanding of language. And, most of the time, we even *reason* metaphorically! "Without metaphor," in fact, "abstract thought is virtually impossible."[4]

After all, metaphor holds "the whole fabric of mental interconnections" together.[5]

So it's no surprise our metaphors also seek deeper levels of meaning. After all, meaning is the very purpose of metaphor. "Metaphor is about life—our life!"[6] And, in our search for greater truths, we

simply push beyond common images to more complex inferences—we reach past basic metaphors to prophetic metaphors.

In the metaphor, "Life is a journey," for example, we transfer all the
rich inferences of journeys to the most intimate events of life.
Without metaphor, in fact, we can't begin to understand the more
profound implications of subjects like "life," "death," or "time."

Clearly, that's the reason metaphor remains basic to all religious
thought. That's why metaphor is becoming an irreplaceable sign in
postmodern theology. And, this explains, as well, why metaphor has
always been, and always will be, the main medium for spiritual
phenomena.

Indeed, metaphor may be the *primary* "Presence" carrier—the
principal Epiphany of reality.

It's been that way since the beginning. Until modern times, metaphor
was seldom considered "unnecessary." In fact, it was the only way
to truly sense ultimate reality. All early visionaries—who pro-
nounced their earth-changing revelations for future generations—moved within metaphor. That's why metaphor served and
continues to serve as the medium of biblical Truth—eternally
forming and informing our belief.

More significant still, metaphor is an "incarnational" language. It is
the "Word made flesh." It molds spiritual realities into recognizable
form. ***Jesus is the ultimate metaphor.*** "He is the exact likeness of
the unseen God [the visible representation of the invisible]."[7]

In short, if we lose metaphor, we have lost Truth.

An Autonomous Source

And, we will lose it if we fail to recognize it. So we must discern the
difference between "dead" metaphors and "live" meta-

phors—between simple metaphors and significant meta-
phors—between common metaphors and complex meta-
phors—between literary metaphors and prophetic meta-
phors—between metaphors of expediency and metaphors of epiphany.

Here's how:

We trace the power in a metaphor to either itself or something *other than* itself. This is essential, for only a prophetic metaphor tran-
scends itself. Only a prophetic metaphor truly passes outside itself, points beyond itself, speaks beyond itself. Its meaning, in other words, exceeds its medium. We realize truth through it, but not in it. It represents something "not there."

It is "virtual." It is "vicarious."

Prophetic metaphor differs from everyday metaphor because it represents a force *independent* of the metaphor—an autonomous Source, full of tension and tendency. Poets don't create metaphors. Metaphors create poets.

We know this removed reality by the shock, the surprise, or the stunned recognition that demands our attention and requires our response. Often, the same prophetic metaphor creates these reactions repeatedly. And, in such moments, the familiar becomes strange and the strange becomes familiar.

Finally, we know the metaphor's hidden, autonomous power by the constraints it places on its own message. Its message does not arrive by chance, it does not spin aimless fantasies in the blue, it does not subject itself to wild subjectivity. We may create or interpret many metaphors, but finally, their messages remain independent of our whimsical intentions.

They have their own way of being.

They move with both compelling and opposing forces. On one hand, metaphoric Truth flows without resistance when we welcome its persuasive power—when we are *inspired,* in other words. On the other hand, metaphor resists *arbitrary* interpretations. For example, a story can't be argued with or dismissed like an idea. And, it's difficult for the teller of a story to twist it totally out of shape.

In other words, metaphor controls its own interpretation. It permits *some*, but not just any, variation. It takes on many forms and lends itself to many interpretations, but—unless completely destroyed—it never loses its intended purpose.

So we recognize the signs of prophetic metaphor when we also recognize the force and control of its message.

———————— ⸙ ————————

Once again, we exist in metaphor. Metaphor meets us where we are. Indeed, God is more real in metaphor than in any previous theology or doctrine. As we increasingly weave the metaphoric web in which we are embedded, we will increasingly witness its signs of Truth.

The future belongs to the language of metaphor—or, more to the point, to the *Presence* of the *Other* within metaphor. And, as that Presence—that "Word"—becomes "flesh," Christ returns to His rightful place in our postmodern world.

Endnotes

1. Lakoff and Johnson, quoted in Fritjof Capra, *The Hidden Connections: Integrating the Biological, Cognitive, and Social Dimensions of Life into a Science of Sustainability* (New York: Doubleday, 2002) p. 63.

2. George Lakoff and Mark Turner, *More than Cool Reason: A Field Guide to Poetic Metaphor* (Chicago: University of Chicago Press, 1989), p. 15, 51.

3. Stephen Pinker, *How the Mind Works* (London: The Softback Preview, 1997) p. 355. See also www.cleanlanguage.co.uk.

4. George Lakoff and Mark Johnson, *Philosophy in the Flesh: The Embodied Mind and Its Challenge to Western Thought* (New York, NY: Basic Books, 1999) pp. 58, 59.

5. Gregory Bateson, quoted in Fritjof Capra, *Uncommon Wisdom: Conversations with remarkable people* (New York: Bantam, 1988) pp 76,77. See also www.cleanlanguage.co.uk.

6. Lewis Edwin Hahn, Editor, *The Philosophy of Paul Ricoeur* (Chicago: Open Court, 1995) p. 271.

7. Colossians 1:15, *The Amplified Bible.*

A Belief-Mosaic

Our search for the language of the future does not end with metaphor. For metaphor links with an even more profound sign of Truth—"pattern recognition." Metaphor finds its greatest depth in *complex* metaphors—*metaphors* of metaphors—*multiple* metaphors—all pointing to the same patterns of Truth. In fact, the more the multiplicity the more the meaning.

We see these signs of Truth in the merging of differing perspectives—in the unity of diverse notions—in a network of manifold meanings—in a system of distinct parts. We recognize these signs when multiple impressions support and corroborate each other—when varied revelations verify and validate each other—when isolated beliefs bring richness and relevance to each other.

And we find these mutual agreements even among mutual disagreements—among apparently contradictory or uncongenial interpretations.

Then, as a result, we sense a greater picture, an integrated whole, a belief-mosaic. Eventually, this mosaic becomes a vast relevance, an overarching pattern, a universal significance. . . .

. . . systems resting within systems—networks nesting within networks.

These patterns of Truth are like holograms where a single part evokes the whole, and the whole is in the part. They are like the Internet where each link leads to the same vast web of relationships. They are like a kaleidoscope where continually changing patterns reflect something that never changes.

They are like a great polyphonic choir where multiple melodies weave soaring similarities and where mingling consonances sound significant because of equally significant dissonances. Or, they are like exquisite choreographies where individual dancers celebrate the same Great Dance.

And, if you are a scientist, these patterns of Truth are like forward-looking physics where previously incompatible theories eloquently converge in one, unified theory of the Universe.

Such patterns are not mere coincidence or serendipitous luck. Nor are they the modern idea of "pattern" where everything reduces to one, exclusive idea. Neither are they the postmodern notion of "pattern" where anything goes. And, finally, they are not the Eastern mysticism of "pattern" where we embrace the whole, but destroy the parts.

Instead, these patterns represent dynamic, flexible systems—worlds teeming with links and minglings. And we're part of them! Again, when whole systems and their parts—including us!—mutually determine one another, they take on powerful and miraculous dimensions.

Yet, paradoxically, these patterns do not reflect many "truths." They reflect One Truth.

The Web of Life

Life is relationship. Wherever we see life, we see patterns or networks of relationships.

And, we know when these connections touch us. An apparent coincidence, as example, may suggest a "bigger picture," consistent and coherent within itself. And we sympathetically respond. We sense a bond between what we feel and something real "out there." Further, we feel at home.

And, moreover, these bonds yield pleasure upon contemplation.

Contrary to modern "logic," this is exactly the way the brain works. The brain's biology demands endless patterns. Or, put another way, this is exactly the way the mind thinks. The mind's versatile and variable nature requires endless links.

Our thinking, in other words, is *meditative*. It is a seemingly random series of serendipitous revelations with multiple feedback loops. We could also describe these loops as "to-and-fro" movements: We think in related images which give light to the whole. Then, increased revelation from the whole gives light to still more related images. Of course, each return or "loop" generates a more complete picture.

This may seem like pandemonium for those who preach a "proper" linear logic. Yet, chaos or information overload "leads to pattern-recognition."[1]

Not surprising, then, this kind of thinking also forms the basis for our beliefs. Faith, after all, is a *mosaic* of belief—a *process* of truth—a *web* of conviction. When our individual convictions support and corroborate each other, our confidence grows. Our faith is affirmed in a myriad of ways, and the affirmations just keep coming.

These affirmations reveal, in turn, a "bigger picture," a greater web of remembering where we know things we didn't know we knew.

> "Every comprehension of a whole
> acknowledges the reality of it."[2]

A "Holy Holograph"

Scripture confirms this pattern recognition, for Scripture is "relational" Truth. Its truths *converge*—its messages *interact*—its "fruit of the Spirit" *relate*.

Granted, Scripture speaks with a multitude of voices—sometimes even contradictory voices. It admits "many-sided wisdom," "infinite variety," and "innumerable aspects."[3] It concedes "many separate revelations," mere "portions" of Truth, and the "different ways" God speaks through the prophets.[4]

Yet, these diverse voices (even conflicting voices) do not mean we've lost the unity or the universal authority of Scripture. For Spirit still speaks with one voice. That's why Paul wrote, "In Him all things consist (cohere, are held together)."[5]

God remains, after all, all in all.

Multiples, mosaics, and many-sided metaphors have more in common with the origin of our faith than with the modern traditions of our culture. Meditative, circular dialogues have more in common with early prophetic voices than with today's production-line ideas. And biblical glory has more in common with the contextual beauty of the first believers than with the intellectual "beauty" of the latest, literal "believers."

God's Kingdom, after all, is a "holy holograph."

> "In many separate revelations [each of which set forth a portion of the Truth] and in different ways God spoke of old to [our] forefathers in and by the prophets."[6]

Pulling Things Together

Pattern recognition—the multilingual voice of God—poses no threat to the minds of the future. For, once again, prophetic voices are seeking signs of Truth in open-ended connections, multiple lines of "reasoning," and interrelated beliefs. They are moving beyond modern signs of "truth"—narrow "truths"—ghettos of "truth."

In doing so, they are pulling things together rather than tearing them apart.

The minds of the future are also moving beyond the postmodern loss of Truth, the shared delusions of subjectivity, and the seas of disconnected dots. In doing so, they are seeing links of significance, connected dots, and the whole in the parts. They are also discovering individual perspectives, unique interpretations, and inspired points of view that are *not* without a Metanarrative—*not* without a Universal Story.

In short, they are discovering the signs of a new "how-we-know" holism—the patterns of a new transcendence—the unity of a new Incarnation.

> "The way we traditionally expressed Christianity may be in trouble, but the future may hold new expressions of Christian faith every bit as effective, faithful, meaningful, and world--transforming as those we've known so far."[7]

Endnotes

1. Marshall McLuhan, quoted in Derrick de Kerckhove, *The Skin of Culture* (Toronto: Somerville House Publishing, 1995) p. 151.

2. Michael Polanyi, *Personal Knowledge: Towards a Post-Critical Philosophy* (Chicago: The University of Chicago Press, 1958) p. 344.

3. Ephesians 3:10, *The Amplified Bible.*

4. Hebrews 1:1, *The Amplified Bible.*

5. Colossians 1:17, *The Amplified Bible.*

6. Hebrews 1:1, *The Amplified Bible*.

7. Brian McLaren, "Emerging Values," *Christianity Today.com*, July 1, 2003   http://www.christianitytoday. com/le/2003/003/3.34.html

A NEW ART

The Seed of Art

The most welcome "emerging" insight has been a new reverence for the role of art. For the language of the future is *damah*—*damah* is metaphor—and metaphor is art.

Hebrew **Damah**—or metaphor—is the foundation of all art. It is the seed of art. It is, in itself, a tiny work of art—a "poem in miniature." Whether images, sounds, objects, gestures, stories, or words, the transcendent tensions between the "known" and the "unknown" within metaphor form the structure of all the arts.

And why not? Hebrew faith and inspired creativity were the same spiritual force. They were one and the same! And that's the reason Hebrew prophets and Hebrew artists were the same spiritual beings. They were also one and the same! We modern Greeks remain erringly arrogant about our arts, but the Hebrews were the only ones who really understood the true role and purpose of art.

Through *damah*, their Creator-God was far more empowering than any Greek theology or doctrine.

And today, in this epic transition, the language of the future returns also to the language of art. Art, as example, is intrinsic to the Internet. It is inherent to the Internet. Both the "infosphere" and the arts are dynamic, intuitive, open-ended systems ruled by invisible forces—forces made sensuous.

Virtual Reality will soon be recognized as a synonym for art.

And, just as the arts layer meaning on top of meaning—mood on top of mood—and mode on top of mode, the Internet is already multi-sensory, multimodal, multimedia, multicultural. . . . Both art and the Internet, in other words, demand our attention on several sensory levels at once.

The definition of this new "technology of art" is found in its ancient origins. The word *tekhne* means "art," and *logia* means "the study of." Truly, art—though often hidden within our technology—has become the *lingua franca* of the future.

This is the transparency we need! This is the turnaround the emerging church requires!

Why? Because art *gets beyond us*. It is the gracious solution to the destructive excess of the emerging church movement. It transcends the pride of mere ideas and the comfort of narrow ideology. It supersedes old apologetics and the worn-out barriers of language. And it bypasses navel-gazing cultures and private property creeds.

Here's how.

Art evokes ever newer modes of meaning and ever newer levels of significance. It calls forth a language beyond language and an incarnation beyond incarnation. And it never stops its meditation with the heart and its communion with Wisdom.

In other words, it's a different way of thinking. Not having answers is more essential than having answers. In fact, the more the ambiguity, the deeper and the more definite the message. Art is usually our only hope when the message is too great or the gap in our understanding is too wide.

It's also a different language. It depends on a pre-semantic surface of our experience for its power—a sphere of "unspoken" realities, "nonverbal" modes, "nonliteral" words. In that sense, it is an *aesthetic* language: evoked more than evaluated—felt more than formulated.

The son of Sirach wrote, for example, "I sought wisdom . . . (and)

She came to me in her beauty."[1]

More important, art can't be argued with or dismissed like a proposition. For it is totally autonomous. It is the only language that manifests its own meaning. So, in its truest form, it is a spiritual language—a Presence carrier—an Epiphany of reality—where Spirit witnesses to spirit. . . .

. . . if only the emerging church could get out of its way! For this is a *different* art. It's not the art emerging leaders embrace.

Their buzzword is "relevance." And some form of relevance is necessary. But most "religious artists"—even "emerging" artists—are about thirty years behind, and they seldom reflect the bold imagination of non-Christian artists. As a result, the "latest" novelties, fads, styles, tastes, and modes are usually dated, dull, repetitious, copycatted and clichéd.

Of course, the "Christian industry" has seized this moment with the least risky business model designed for the most spiritually bankrupt masses. Even "cutting edge" artists in the darker worlds of punk rock have added a few religious words for a few religious dollars. But something "cutting edge" can become an overnight cliché just as quickly as some creaky old coot.

Hidden behind these mistaken efforts is the ever present need to feed the flesh. And this is okay too. But often, "emerging art" feeds the flesh more than it feeds the faith. Unbelievably, it assumes an "anointing" for our more seductive urges, pent-up passions, and clever cartharses.

This art is a turned-in, self-reflecting, soulish art.

Finally, there are those who worship "high art," "fine art," "cultured art," or "great art"—where the power in art is supposedly found within art itself. But their "good taste" mistakes the oyster for the pearl. For, finally, the meaning in art transcends the metaphor in art. Art may be a means to life more abundant, but it is not—in itself—life more abundant.

My apology to all those wannabe "esthetes."

So whether the arts are popularly relevant, fleshly rewarding, or even culturally refined, they must first prove themselves to be live metaphors—then prophetic metaphors. They must flow with a metaphoric language common to all the arts yet flourishing beyond the arts.

But metaphor is not possible without emotion, so we also discern the feelings beyond our knee-jerk emotions in the natural world. We discern the veracity of an "experienced" Truth, a "felt" Truth, a "vicarious" (not-us) Truth.

Obviously, this art is neither of us nor by us. And, its message is neither metaphor nor emotion. It is, instead, an intuitive system ruled by invisible forces. We can only point out of the power to which we point.

Especially important for emerging leaders, this art is not limited to specific times and places or the usual disciplines of music, poetry, dance, drama, or visual art. For the art of the future will occur anytime, anyplace, in any form, and on several levels at once. In other words, art is leaping outside itself. It's breaking the barriers between art and life itself. What we once called "art" is showing up incognito in endless evoked events.

The "art" is never noticed. Only the power.

Few emerging leaders, though, show the spiritual skills for this art. Few reveal its inspired craftsmanship. Few bring mature artistry to the Voice of the Spirit.

So we need a return of poets/prophets who knowingly become walking parables, transforming presences, vital virtual realities—extracting the precious from the worthless—making all things sacred. We need emerging leaders who "are not so much describing the world as creating a new one."[2]

Damah will become the primary tongue of our time—the most powerful force in history—the next "incarnation" of our faith. . . .

. . . and its "art" will become our ultimate communion.

> ". . . and to God . . . thanks, who at *all* times is leading us in triumph in the Christ, and the fragrance of His knowledge He is manifesting *through us in every place*."[3]

Endnotes

1. Sirach 51:13, 14 *The New American Bible.*

2. William Irwin Thompson, *Coming Into Being* (New York: St. Martin's Press, 1996) p. 153.

3. II Corinthians 2:14, *Young's Literal Translation.*

The "Coin of the Realm"

So the most significant moment in art is upon us. With astounding new forms, the arts are becoming the "coin of the realm." Of course, art—and language—constantly change. But today's change proves a singular watershed event.

What are the forces driving this change?

Any historic shift—like the present shift from the modern to the postmodern world—stirs new visions and rids old obstacles. And, such daring constantly breaks barriers. Then, these broken barriers nurture new arts.

But metaphor mainly drives today's change. Metaphor is the prophetic power in the future of language, and the future of language is the prophetic promise in the future of art. For, finally, metaphor is the seed of all art.

Of course, our rush toward an oral culture (where vision exceeds logic) feeds this promise, as well. For art is endemic to an oral culture.

These are the forces, but what do they mean? What will we do when we don't do what we're doing now? The leaders of the emerging church *must answer*!

Useless Arts

To understand the present, we must understand the past—especially our biased Greek past.

Old cultural leaders with both feet firmly fixed in an old cultural world claim "art has nothing to do with meaning"[1]—that it "asserts nothing"[2]—that it is finally "useless."[3] Even in the church! "For much of Christian history, educators and theologians have expressed a deep suspicion of the arts."[4] St. Augustine insisted that truth is always "disembodied and purely intellectual."[5] And the modern theologian Karl Barth agreed, "Beauty is a risky concept." Its pleasure "should not, therefore, be associated with the serious business of religion."[6]

Of course, we pay lip service to the "sacred" arts.

We have allowed the popular arts to cook the moods in market-driven churches. We have valued art as decor in the same way we value wall-to-wall carpeting. And, we have admired even the "fine arts," though we refuse any notion of their carrying final meanings. No matter the contrary beliefs, seldom has the modern world known art as an instrument of Truth.

And with good reason. Art has been forced to serve the "reality"—the logic and science—of the modern world. And, beyond a useless, abstract beauty, no other means to "truth" has been allowed. So, in the absence of sacred aesthetics or a theology of art, church leaders have long surmised that the arts share a bed with cheap and empty "sentiment."

As a result, meaning in the arts has long been lost to logical "sophistication" and artless commercialization.

A New Apologetic

Not anymore. A new art supersedes old apologetics and brings new proofs of Truth.

In a world where the doctrines of truth and goodness struggle to survive, beauty and art still connect with culture. While visionary youth refuse the limited language and pious paraphrases of the past, they still yearn to know the message of beauty—the meaning in art.

And, where modern minds seek reality through scientific analysis, other minds seek *ultimate* reality through sensuous art.

In short, allowed and disallowed knowledge are crossing in ways that excite artists and upset academics. But the artists are winning!

Cutting edge scientists, for example, appeal to poetry. Itzhak Bentov describes the universe as "a vibrating, dancing organism." He says, in fact, "the universe as a whole and we in particular are not matter, but music."[7]

And scholars join these forces, when

> the novelist becomes a prophet, the composer a magician, and the historian a bard, a voice recalling ancient identities.[8]

Even theologians leave their libraries to mix with musicians, actors, artists, poets and dancers. Indeed, a future theology may never appear in text books. It may, instead, be painted, sculpted, danced, performed, crafted. . . .

Of course, the notion of art "arguing truth" doesn't make sense in any excellence of logic. And the "apologetics of art" shows a silliness beyond all rules of credibility. But we're talking about a different excellence and a new credibility. We're pointing to a different way of meaning what we mean and a new way of signifying what is significant.

After all, art delivers meaning in an entirely different way from logical discourse. *The disciplines achieving perfection in one will not attain results in the other.*

Let's get beyond this silliness.

Instead of fixed ideas or precise points of view, art requires a *non*rational sense for its power—a sense that lies deeper than "exact" thought. Instead of locking down final "truth," art moves with cryptic poignancy, rich ambiguity, and puzzling paradox. And, instead of one literal answer, art yields meaning from multiple views and endless patterns.

Instead of cold, objective "truth," art explores privately felt meanings. Instead of predictable arguments, art surprises us with the unpredictable. And, instead of step-by-step conclusions (like lawyers before a jury), art suddenly transports us to new perspectives.

The Otherwise Unknown

Art proves many vantages in its "knowing."

For art reveals the otherwise unknown. It works beyond the edge of easy knowing. Indeed, it is the only way we find God's creative presence in history.[9] For art breaks through the crust of formal thinking. It sets aside the world of untrue believing.

It is a music you never would have known to listen for.

In the art of Virtual Reality, for example, we see still another "real" world. For in art we confront the "ultimately real."[10] We see beyond the limits of a psychological world, for art looks past both subjectivity and objectivity. And, we see beyond man's boxed-in "isms," for true art is not the private property of any man's creed.

We see beyond the warmed-over truth and reinvented "wheels" of the past, for art reveals the totally new. We see beyond the illness of culture, for art transcends culture. And we see beyond even art itself, for art points beyond itself.

Seeing beyond such things, "personal" vision proves another advantage of "knowing" in the arts. After all, all we do, we do in order to "feel" its significance. And art serves a valid vision of this significance. It is both intimate and ultimate. As it penetrates, permeates, and impresses us, it illuminates, seizes, and motivates us.

It is the reality of "truth felt."

More important, art is a "transforming" knowing. Far stronger than mere data, it recreates us, changes us, and transforms us. Bach believed music "recreates the human spirit." Beethoven wrote, "Anyone who understands my music is saved." The author Doestoevsky insisted, "Beauty will save the world." And the theologian Tillich claimed a Botticelli painting changed his whole life.

As the arts drop their old "decor" roles, they will form the new apologetic, the new proof of Truth. Then, preachers will become artists—masters of the story. And artists will become preachers—masters of the "Word."

A Degenerate Priesthood?

Of course, I'm talking about true art, art that surpasses art—not the abuse or misuse of art.

Art meant only to entertain—seductive, popular, and indulgent—feeds the flesh more than it feeds the faith. And its products and producers, with profit margins in mind, *exert power over* their customers rather than *give power to* their customers. On a less harmful level, the same vendors sell mere "decor" arts—art we can do with or without. The music in malls and dairy farms, for example, flows languidly with a passive and timeless reverie. But its manipulated moods merely "milk" the shoppers as well as the dairy cows.

More "cultured" arts dwell in refined schools where privileged status and prevailing standards pay homage to the great heros and triumphs of culture. At these altars, art usually exists for the sake of art—it points only to itself. We may be ravished by its beauty, but we remain the same. Or, with more pride, we say, "Art is about the artist." Art, in other words, glorifies the artist.

These arts, pulled lose from deeper and truer origins, wander the moral landscape with no conviction. And—sooner or later—they prove helpless against the demonic. Much of today's art, for example, flaunts a stylish pessimism or an angry cynicism. Some say, "In our postmodern era, the artists have become a degenerate priesthood."[11]

> "Woe unto those who . . . have lyre
> and harp, tambourine and flute . . . but
> they do not regard the deeds of the
> Lord."[12]

Referential Power

Still, art *can* speak Truth.

To begin, we live in a symbolic world. Always, "The fundamental gestures of existence bear a *symbolic potential*."[13] And in that potential, all events "surpass their appearance."[14] In other words, we live in a metaphoric world more than a "real" world.

Our metaphoric world is a linguistic world of "unspoken" realities and nonverbal modes. Hidden under supposedly arbitrary words lurk the stories of our culture in all their glory and vainglory. And, concealed behind the lie of modern "objectivity" hide the events of Truth in all their closure and disclosure.

In this hidden world, language is possible only with metaphor. If we lose the referential power of metaphor—the ability to represent hidden realities—we have lost truth, culture, and life itself. We have also lost art, for metaphor and art are identical twins.

So we can say, then, art also "speaks." It reveals, discloses, testifies.

The early church knew this. The whole drama of salvation was played out in visual images. Pope Gregory the Great said, "Images are for unlettered beholders what scripture is for the reader."[15] And a later church council affirmed, "What the gospel tells us by words, the icon proclaims by colors."[16]

In the same way, a future proof of truth increases the role of our senses, emotions, and feelings, for you cannot have metaphor without them. So a new credibility will demand new standards of honesty and excellence in perceiving truth through the body.

Art, then, destines to become a new "incarnation" of our faith. The great poet Goethe warned that art is "no mere amusement to charm the idle or relax the careworn." Instead, it is the "sister of religion."[17] And Albert Schweitzer echoed, "All true and deeply felt music, whether sacred or profane, journeys to heights where art and religion can always meet."[18]

So life, language, metaphor, art, and emotion—they all speak Truth. And the language of the future will know their sisterhood.

Starting a "Clean Slate"

But the promises of the past require radically different arts for the future. And the art forms of the future alter most of what we've known from the art forms of the past. True, postmodern trends may resemble passing fads, but we hear rumblings in these trends that echo historic changes. Indeed, it presages the shaking of a whole new paradigm for the arts.

Surprisingly, this should not surprise. Art simply resonates to deep changes in our culture—to the way we think—to our grasp of reality. And, as we move away from a white, European, "enlightened," male-dominated culture, we also discover our wrong ideas about the arts.

As a result, we feel a growing unease with the old definitions, strict recipes, and logical limits of art. We sense a widening distance with a one-size-fits-all, "thinking-man's" musing. And, we question the produced, programmed, and professional arts of an out-of-step elderly elite.

Even arts for the masses catch our questions. More and more we distrust the canned, commercial arts neutered of all that prevents sales to the widest possible market. So we are, indeed, redefining the "mass" in "mass markets."

In this new decade of a new century, the arts are starting with a "clean slate."

Radical Metaphors

Again, metaphor has always been basic to art. And the paradox between the "unknown" and the "known" has always been basic to metaphor. But now, the widest gap between past and future bears witness to a new and fearless push toward paradox—toward a *radical* metaphor.

Today, for example, we show a voracious appetite for juxtaposition, enigma, collage, and just plain hodgepodge. We have suddenly redoubled our ability to combine diverse things in impossible ways. And we have brazenly inflated our affinity for comparing the incomparable—for placing side by side the incompatible.

We all take part in this "extreme" game. And—in doing so—all of us question the old orders of veracity while stumbling blindly and boldly toward evermore bizarre sources of meaning.

And, as we could expect, bizarre metaphors show up in a world of "multi-everything" arts. Multimedia, multimodal, multicultural, multisensory, multifaceted, multilayered. . . . Meanings on top of meanings, moods on top of moods, modes on top of modes. . . .

Like a hall of mirrors, they demand our attention on several levels at once.

"Techno worship," for example, blurs the borders between music, poetry, dance, drama, visual art, the event itself, and all the senses—all at the same time! Given enough bandwidth, digital science can simultaneously engage all of our senses. And it can do this in ways to which the older arts can only hint. As example, crossing quickly from one sense to the other, we move beyond the old notion that the arts are sensory specific—that "music is for the ear," "visual art is for the eye," and so on.

This "multi-everything" world—this ambiguity of polyphony—will only increase the depth of the message. It will prove a perfect haven for powerful prophetic metaphors.

Losing Our Timeline

As if it were possible, future arts will also bow before a new time and space.

The "timeline" arts—arts that take place over time (like music)—were heavily shaped by the linear, serial logic of the Enlightenment. Classical symphonies, for example, took a musical "idea," then developed it over a timeline. That idea had to "go somewhere." It had to "do something." It had to show a logical exposition, development, and conclusion. And, the dramatic interplay between these carefully sequenced moods birthed the musical classics of our culture.

Yet today, many listeners want more than clock-like events hooked together like "beads on a string." Their druthers should be obvious: *As thoughts lose their logical sequence, the performing arts lose their "timeline."* These arts begin to work more in "realtime," focusing on the moment itself. They become, in other words, more "vertical" and less "horizontal."

Today's pop culture reflects these transient, "realtime" moments. Recent books, for example, present endless incoherent and isolated episodes. Leading theaters stage random streams of consciousness. And, even the illusion of films pastes together mere fragments of filed-away film clips.

In music, these event-character "moments" more and more take on the quality of immobile "paintings." These moments differ from the music of the past where moods followed each other like ducks in a row. Today, for example, a whole gamut of moods—like struggle, assurance, and celebration—can pile onto each instant, the way paintings present complete pictures at each glance.

Or, listen to the realtime, "ambient" music of today's youth. Their "chilling out" music presents contemplative "soundscapes," the way an older painting presents romantic "landscapes." These sound-scapes, however, "stand still" more by endlessly repeated patterns than by simultaneous moods. Such contemplation surfaces from a going-nowhere, mood music made of short, cyclical, and simple, chantlike phrases.

Similar examples include Taize music[19] and New Age music.

By classical standards, many label this music a poverty-stricken creativity. Yet, those who contemplate these sounds say the sheer simplicity never gets boring. Instead, it grows ever deeper, forming something within that was not there before. These endlessly recurring sounds give listeners the chance to become completely "lost" in the music.

Yes, these sounds open the door to something. The question is what? We should recall that the spiritual realm has a fork in the road.

In summary, we are moving toward a new time and space in the arts.

But, between now and then, the performing arts will hold the metaphoric tensions between both minutes and moments, form and freedom, progress and pattern, going somewhere and going nowhere. . . .

Where all this ends? Nobody knows.

Personal Art

History boldly rejects still another idea about the arts. We have ended the notion that art exists only for itself—that it parades excellence only for its sake. Recent history reveals less regard for the restricted arts of the cultural elite—the "educated" arts—the "mind" arts.

We are savoring a distaste for mere "good taste."

So we move, at the same time, toward a more "personal" art—toward the importance of *all* participants, their secret pleasure, their firsthand experience. After all, art was never meant to be separated from life. In addition, today's need for ratings and sales in the marketplace demands an inclusive audience rather than an elite few.

Music for a larger audience, however, doesn't require a loss of depth or profundity. It simply demands a revivified directness—a specific message to a specific person at a specific time.

We see this in-your-face directness in the "alternative worship" arts of today's youth. Intimate and honest, these arts exude a risk-taking, freewheeling worship. Their "hip-hop" ecstasies grow from a life style of rap, break dancing, and graffiti. And their "rave" raptures grow into a euphoric marathon of all-night dancing.

This is the art of our earliest origins.

No wonder. The agelong quest for the secret intimacy between beauty and meaning has turned suddenly into a headlong rush toward senses and emotions. As a result, pop culture citizens are now ardent collectors of felt meanings and emotional kicks.

And, we haven't yet seen the final fruit! For science will revision our senses. It will create sensual images that today's arts can only begin to suggest. The freedom to probe a "biological" art—grounded in feelings and emotions—will find new and amazing sensory expressions. In fact, a new "tech-art" will extend our senses, like quickened prostheses.[20]

And it will provide more depth than any previous art.

Interactive Art

Another seismic change in the arts bursts from the new "interface culture." It brings a tidal wave shift from passive spectators in the arts to active players in the arts. And it reveals itself to us through cyberspace, which, again, "reveals itself to us only through . . . interface design."[21]

This interface design "is the great *symbolic* accomplishment of our era."[22] Cyberspace, after all, is an immensely disordered realm ruled by invisible forces. It requires the sensuous gestures—the "interface"—of icons, links, and metaphors to imagine this infinity and to restore a feeling of order. And these symbols run exactly parallel to the sense-making interface in both religion and art.

In short, the Internet "interface" *is* art:

> (The Internet) is now emerging—chrysalis-style—as a genuine art form . . . as complex and vital as the novel or the cathedral or the cinema . . . (it is) perhaps *the* art form of (this) century.[23]

That's the reason digital gurus often resemble priests and prophets.

For they are the "artisans" of an interface culture. And that's the reason all postmodern citizens are born to prophesy. For the new world of interface requires indigenous, interactive, Internet arts—warts and all.

> "When I think about the gap between
> raw information and its numinous life
> on the screen . . . the whole sensation
> has a strangely religious feel to it."[24]

Endnotes

1. The British philosopher Harold Osborne, editor of the *British Journal of Aesthetics*, quoted in *Religious Aesthetics: A Theological Study of Making and Meaning* by Frank Burch Brown (Princeton, New Jersey: Princeton University Press, 1989) p. 26.

2. R. G. Collingwood, quoted in Louis Dupré, *Symbols of the Sacred* (Grand Rapids: Eerdmans, 2000) pp. 72, 73.

3. Paul Valery, quoted in Nicholas Wolterstorff, *Art in Action: Toward a Christian Aesthetic* (Grand Rapids, Michigan: William B. Eerdmans Publishing Company, 1980) p. 3.

4. Frank Burch Brown, "Characteristics of Art and the Character of Theological Education," *Theological Education*, Volume XXXI, Number 1, Autumn 1994, p. 7.

5. St. Augustine, quoted in Brown.

6. Karl Barth, quoted in Patrick Sherry, *Spirit and Beauty: An Introduction to Theological Aesthetics* (Oxford: Clarendon Press, 1992) p. 21.

7. Itzhak Bentov, quoted in Barbara Bullard, "The Road to Remembrance," *The Monroe Institute, 1995 http://www.monroeinstitute.com*

/voyages/hsj-1995-winter-remembrance-bullard.html

8. William Irwin Thompson, *The Time Falling Bodies Take to Light: Mythology, Sexuality, and the Origins of Culture* (New York: St. Martin's Press, 1981) p. 4.

9. We find this idea in Plato, Aristotle, Dante, Spenser, Handel, Haydn, Kant, Jaspers, Ricoeur, Whitehead, Dewey, Heidegger, and countless other artists and thinkers.

10. Louis Dupré, *Symbols of the Sacred* (Grand Rapids: Eerdmans, 2000) p. 71.

11. Thompson, p. 248.

12. Isaiah 5:11, 12; *The Amplified Bible*.

13. Louis Dupré, pp. 122, 123.

14. Dupré.

15. Pope Gregory, quoted in Sally Morgenthaler, *Sacramentis*, 2005 http://www.sacramentis.com/articles/text/misc./wipc2.html (At the publication of this book, her site had been closed.)

16. Eighth Ecumenical Council, quoted in Morgenthaler, *Sacramentis* (above).

17. Goethe, quoted in Arianna Stassinopoulos, *After Reason* (New York: Stein and Day, 1978), p. 157.

18. Albert Schweitzer, quoted in "Through the Ages," *Music of the Soul*, April 15, 2006 http://www.musicofthesoul.com/through_the _ages.htm

19. Taize is a village in France with an ecumenical community.

Their simple, chant-like meditative music, written mostly by the monk Jacques Berthier, appeals especially to international youth.

20. Derrick de Kerckhove, *The Skin of Culture* (Toronto: Somerville House Publishing, 1995) p. 86.

21. Steven Johnson, *Interface Culture: How New Technology Transforms the Way We Create and Communicate* (New York: Basic Books, 1997) p 19.

22. Johnson, pp 212-215.

23. Johnson, pp 212-215, 238-242.

24. Johnson, pp 212-215.

A NEW INTEGRITY

Lightning Bugs Or Lightning?

The Lord of History has created "a perfect storm" for all *spiritual* leaders. He has forcefully redefined spiritual leadership, and it's all for the good.

To begin, the way we "know"—or, the way we discover new "ways" of knowing—is continually changing. And, in the next 50 years this "knowing" will change more than in the last 400 years.[1] The latest scientific methods, for example, no longer remove the observer from the observation.[2] The "subjective"—that is, intuition and instinct, feeling and faith, meditation and emotion—has become a "scientific" necessity![3]

Suddenly, this necessity reveals new levels of meaning. And, undoubtedly, the Holy Spirit will be involved. Computers, for example, increasingly provide a real-time, spontaneous, fluid, meditative, "feedback" way of knowing. And in this space-age mysticism, open-ended possibilities are expanding the Mystery faster than we can understand it. Yet, within our embryonic understanding, we are discovering a new "network" of truth, an enormous "pattern" of truth, a god-like Universe of truth.

Honoring the ancient Hebrews, we are finally admitting that all things exist in the invisible realm before they appear in the visible realm. More to the point, most emerging church leaders are on a collision course with the Holy Spirit, and either they move with history or they'll know the rightful warning of a great shaking.

Spiritual leadership assumes *spiritual* leadership—but among most "spiritual" leaders, we can't assume that.

Their mentors in our seminaries, for example, know how to have integrity of the mind, but seldom integrity of the Spirit. They write and talk about the Spirit, but seldom encounter the Spirit. They hold dear their "theology" of the Spirit, but seldom the "demonstration" of the Spirit. The scholarly elite willingly write on events, but avoid events writing on them. They walk confidently in the grammatical, but avoid the mystical. And, they display skill in the literal, but avoid the metaphorical.

As a result, God's "manifest presence" remains a mere idea—miracles cause major embarrassment—and the "empowering" of the unempowered triggers terror. These scholars know how to "upload" earth to heaven, but they don't know how to "download" heaven to earth.

There's a difference, after all, between intellectual sophistication and spiritual integrity—invented ideas and revealed visions—informed opinions and prophetic insights. There's a divergence between outward inventions and inward gestations—conjectural faith and indelible faith—the charisma of a person and the Person of a charisma. There's a dissimilarity between delivering information and receiving revelation—the manipulating of "spirit" and the motivating of Spirit—or "spiritual authority" and the authority of the Spirit.

In the words of Mark Twain, that difference is the difference between a "lightning bug" and "lightning."[4]

So the Spirit is everything emerging leaders are not! After all, an encounter with the Spirit is an encounter with the "Not-Us." It makes its own way, not our way. It has an "Is-ness" long before we try to give form to that "Is-ness." That's why we bump into the strange within the familiar, the extraordinary within the ordinary, the other world within this world. And that's why so many of our moments are broken into—why so often our status quo is transformed.

We sense the Spirit in self-evident "signs" that reveal power. We find it in the endless portals of paradox that open onto the profound facts within profound fictions. Or, more to the point, we find it

whenever the "Word becomes flesh."   Then, empowered passions—quickening influences—and impelling forces carry us along
as in a great river.

Or, by analogy, muscles move those who "pump iron," but hidden
powers propel the ecstatic dancer.

How do we find that power? How do we allow it? How do we
participate in it? What are the definitions?—the guidelines? In short,
how do we strike such a colossal "tuning fork."[5]

It's certainly not by what we've been doing—flying blind with a
cereal box compass. Leaders can no longer follow their old eclectic,
do-your-own-thing spirituality.   They can no longer leave their
experiences "untested, undiscerned, and ungrounded."[6] And they can
no longer tell their followers, "Just trust me!"

Because we're moving into lands where our best maps no longer
apply. In short, we've lost our ability to verify spiritual integrity
within a postmodern world. The Spirit hasn't changed, but the way
we discern the Spirit has changed.

So we must re-establish grounds of credibility. We must learn to
discern the veracity of our sense experiences—the "utterances of true
spirits and false ones"[7]—and the enigmatic mysteries within
metaphor. For "the Spirit of the living God" is written on "tablets of
human hearts"—not the blackboards of intellectual minds.[8]

Yet, it is painfully difficult for emerging leaders to get beyond the
culture that created them. How sorrowful it is to be weighed down
with a mere propositional "Spirit" and a life-long suspicion of
"beyond-the-logic-of-the-mind" religion. Many desperate leaders
want to make this change, but sometimes it seems impossible.

This journey requires humble risk and profound courage—and
probably the guidance of a mentor. But when Spirit takes on body

and body takes on Spirit, what could be more important?

The emerging church doesn't need any more "powerful" leaders. It needs more leaders with prophetic power. For "The Spirit is the author of the world."[9] All of us, at heart, are living manifestations—contingent realities—reciprocal agents. And we are driven to unload the resulting passion in the brief breath of our history.

Yet, we must also learn from history. The monastic movement—a movement of spiritual integrity—saved the church. And, today—for the first time in history—we are being offered not only the integrity of the mind, but the integrity of the spirit as well.

"Woe to . . . those who prophesy out of their own mind."[10]

Endnotes

1. Kevin Kelly, "The Scientific Method," *Google TechTalks*, May 9, 2006, http://video.google.com/videoplay?docid=-6119231548215342323

2. Studies on the origin of the Universe and on quantum mechanics provide examples.

3. See also the new study of "epigenetics." Our free will—resulting, for example, from "beautiful music," "great art," and other subjectivity—is not only real, it can actually override our DNA. "Suddenly, epigenetically caused gene expression is as much if not more important than the genes themselves." Scientists have also proven that today's personal decisions can affect the genes of later generations as well. From: Benjamin Wiker, "How You Live Your Life Matters," *ToTheSource*, November 22, 2006 http://www.tothesource.org/11_22_2006/ 11_22_ 2006.htm

4. Paraphrasing a Mark Twain quote at Barbara Schmidt, "Directory of Mark Twain's maxims, quotations, and various opinions,"

TwainQuotes, April 9, 1997 http://www.twainquotes.com/Light ning.html

5. Leonard Sweet, quoted in Peter Walker and Tyler Clark, "Missing the Point?" *Relevant Magazine*, Issue 21, July-August, 2006, pp 70-74.

6. Gordon D. Fee, *Paul, the Spirit, and the People of God* (Peabody, Massachusetts: Hendrickson Publishers, 1996) p. 188.

7. I Corinthians 12:1-10, *Amplified Bible*.

8. II Corinthians 3:3, *Amplified Bible*.

9. Grenz and Franke, *Beyond Foundationalism: Shaping Theology In A Postmodern Context* (Louisville: Westminster John Knox Press, 2001) p.77.

10. Ezekiel 13:2, 3; *Amplified Bible*.

Spiritual Leadership?

There's no way we can talk about *tomorrow's* spiritual leaders out of *today's* context. For tomorrow's spiritual leaders are "unthinkable"—they can't be defined by either past or present concepts. Here, for example, are a few leaders who will probably be left behind:

"Milquetoast Pastors" Passive leaders are usually "called" to a congregation rather than to a mission. They're led entirely by their board and other "controllers." Many of these dear souls are burned-out or disillusioned church reformers. Others are desperately "co-dependent," hoping to serve out their modest assignments.

"Churchy Clergy" Career-driven clergy reach the pinnacle of their achievement when they are ordained by the ordained. These "officially" anointed Christians draw their esteem from the entitlements of their "certification." And they love top-down religiosity, spiritual bureaucracies, and legalistic agendas.

"Hospital Chaplains" Chaplain churches are like hospitals where people are healed, protected, and comforted. In these churches, though, the shepherd never leads his sheep beyond their protected enclosure. Pastoral care is the pastor's *only* ministry. And his message is always the same, "Take two aspirin and go to bed."

"Information Brokers" These preachers are teachers. They impart "knowledge," deliver "information," and mediate the "facts" of faith. Academic credentials and proper theologies are their primary imperatives. These "thinkers" teach us how to think, but seldom how to live. They give us "just the facts, Mam"—then we're on our own.

"Ministry Police" These guardians "do" the ministry. The laity may serve on committees or do minor stuff, but these "professionals" *are* the ministry. It's a caste system, a clear divide between those who are "official" and those who are "just lay persons." So, "Keep in your place and don't get in the way."

"Control Freaks" Command-and-control clergy belong to the same family as the "Ministry Police." They micromanage the whole church and insist on approving everything. The laity, of course, must do exactly what they're told, for errors are seldom forgiven.

"Feudal Overlords" These kingdom builders ("kingdom" with a small "k") are mostly concerned about the size and resources of their church. This makes sense, for their church is conspicuously *about them*. Though "The Son of man came not to be waited on but to serve,"[1] these "overlords" are motivated, instead, by the privileges of position and power.

"Marketing CEO's" Many "managers of the sacred" are also marketing experts. They covet the powers of strategic planning and commercial success. Their game is a numbers game, so whatever the market wants. . . . These pastors harvest where nothing is planted. They barter a spiritual birthright for something "far more successful."

———————————— ∞∞∞●∞∞∞ ————————————

Does the Lord still love these guys? Of course!

Yet. . . . The church needs leaders. *Spiritual* leaders. Especially today! For increasingly, our world is a "Sorcerer's Apprentice" world where powerful changes are moving beyond our control.

This looming crisis is more than the apocalypse of rampant technology—more than the drunken indulgence of a new paganism—more than the demonic quicksands of secular spiritualism—more than the virtual insanity of virtual reality—more than the nihilist networking of global guerrillas. . . .

It's the critical mass of all these—and more!

Not What We Expect

No wonder the church feels paralyzed. In addition to the many flawed roles among today's clergy, the Lord of History demands new roles that seem impossible for us to grasp. Among the leaders of the emerging church, these roles are often opposite of what we expect. For the *spiritual* leaders of the future are antithetical, paradoxical, enigmatic—*totally out-of-the-box*!

For any visionary—serious enough to become one of the "new spiritual leaders"—risks the stigma that comes from a life *beyond* "proper" churches, *beyond* "respectable" seminaries, and *beyond* the "politically correct" rules of most emerging church leaders.

Without apology, I offer the following visions of the new man or woman of God:

"An Otherworldly Visitor" Though totally normal, he explores the edges of normalcy. Though typically intuitive, he travels the frontiers of the counterintuitive. And, though cognizant of the possible, he embraces the impossible.

He feels totally comfortable with ludicrous contradictions and ridiculous juxtapositions. He believes that when he is weak, he is strong—when he is a slave, he is free—when he is humbled, he is exalted.[2]   He lives a life bold, yet humble—confident, yet self-effacing—powerful, yet subtle—single minded, yet open.

And, not far from the bizarre, he is "both called and empowered to be an extension of the Incarnation"[3]—a living, breathing "Word made flesh"![4] Of course, society's reactions to such "arrogant illusions" would not have surprised St. Paul, for his own converts were embarrassed and scandalized by similar off-the-wall statements.

"A Maverick" Though willing to work within the strictures of structure, he is—at heart—a free spirit, a nonconformist. For his vision of God's Kingdom is constrained neither by worn-out conventions, blind commitments, nor cultural bias.

He's not interested, for example, in the worst manifestations of "being religious." He's not interested in the barnacles of past cultures that still burden other leaders. And, he's not interested in the latest goals and gods of secular success.

Instead, he's interested in the epic "moves" of a "moving" Lord of History. He's interested in a spiritual integrity that embraces a new—yet, far more profound—orthodoxy. And, he's interested in quality rather than quantity—the promises of a distant, yet greater, harvest.

As example, this "careful cowboy" does "triage" on his own followers—maximizing his influence on those who *want* to grow, those who *want* to lead, those who *want* to become spiritual entrepreneurs of a global, networking world.

"A Nobody" A radically selfless leader, he *believes* the hard sayings of Jesus. He accepts failure, crisis, and hardship as the secret of his success. He practices giving up his life with the full expectation of his life being given back again.

Everybody else, of course, wants to be loved, accepted, and appreciated. That's normal and necessary. But this transfigured being willingly forgoes being "somebody." Like St. Paul, who stepped down from a world of status and prominence, this transcendent spirit knows a similar ridicule and rejection.

More to the point, he has given up a leader-centered ministry for a lay-centered ministry. He has given up receiving accolades for giving accolades. And, he has given up making himself successful for making others successful.

In other words, he has forfeited turf-protection for mentoring and networking. He has forfeited personal ownership for empowering others. And, he has forfeited quick "notches on his salvation 'gun belt'" for caring and lasting relationships.

"A Risk-Taker" The first rule of "responsible" church leadership is simple and sane: "Don't rock the boat." It's also the second, third, and fourth rules. So the daredevil deeds of church pioneers are really not worth the risk. They don't make good sense.

True enough. Church leaders should be profoundly cautious.

Yet, anyone truly led by the Lord will willingly risk *responsible spontaneity*. They will risk—in the same moment!—the awe within the ordinary, the mystery within the mundane, the numinous within the natural, and the intuitive within the intellect.

And, with a "wild patience," they will risk even careful chaos. For they've learned that the miraculous transitions of unwelcome chaos are far more empowering than the comfortable retreats of an overly prudent peace.

"A Foreign Language Fanatic" This man of God prefers an "other" language, an *intentionally* ambiguous and obscure parlance. His delivery often resembles "sign language"—closer, perhaps, to "doubletalk" or "doublespeak" than logical discourse. Among most emerging leaders, of course, such "language" is nonsense.

No wonder. This new leader has changed from charted logic to uncharted "logic"—from a literal world to a metaphorical world—from facts to phenomena. He has changed from dead metaphors to live metaphors—from proofs to paradox—from consistent patterns to juxtapositions. And, he has changed from exaggerated control to "controlled exaggeration"—from rhetorical flair to transcendent revelation—from a "real" world to a Virtual Reality world.

He knows and practises "straight" language. Yet, he also knows "God writes straight with crooked lines."[5]

"An Artist" In a life of endless role changes, he has shifted from a dry theologian to an inspired artist—from a manager to a poet—from a pious presence to a prophetic presence. For he's totally convinced he was created in the image of a Creative God.

So his empowered purpose now reflects a life of *serious* "make-believe." In this, he follows the commands of Scripture: He continually "makes offers the Holy Spirit can't refuse." He "calls things that are not as though they were."[6] And he gives creative form to the "substance," "evidence" and "proof" of things we do not see.[7]

He is boldly *proactive*.

And, in the process, he births the precious within the worthless. He gives form to the Word within the flesh. And, he midwifes Divine power within the poor and powerless.

"A Pathfinder" This sensitive explorer leaves the "approved" highways and looks for the hidden byways. He sets aside the old role of a doctrinal guide and assumes the new role of a tour guide. No longer does he say, "Do as I say." Now, he says, "Do as I do."

He may temporarily suspend his analytical mind, yet his awareness reaches an even higher alertness. He never loses the integrity of his mind, yet he is led by the even greater integrity of his spirit. He always excels in talking "about" God and "to" God, yet—far more important—he crosses the forbidden border and lets God talk too.

In other words, he's always "On the Way." With watchful expectancy, he looks for the unseen. With intense obedience, he listens for the Lord of History.

And his obedience manifests a peculiar paradox. He leads, yet he is led—he speaks "in-your-face," yet "in-His-grace"—he's dauntless, yet docile. He's blind, yet he sees—he moves with faithful uncertainty, yet he knows the certainty of his faith—he doesn't know where he's going, yet always gets to where God wants him to go.

In other words, he is both proactive and reactive—creating and submitting, active and passive, doing and being, speaking and listening, answering and asking. . . .

. . . all in the same moment!

Errors of Pride

In the modern world, none of the above traits are "normal"—none of them are "logical"—none of them deal with our notion of "reality." Yet, for those willing to explore this new world, typical errors remain:

Contrary to opinion, none of these traits requires "talent." Even those at the top of the "food chain"—the educated and sophisticated, prestigious and powerful, charismatic and clever, glib and gifted—provide no "added glory." Still, fleshly confusion remains between inspiration and invention—intuition and problem solving—vision and product—calling and accomplishment.

In other words, the heroic narcissism of human leadership is grossly overrated.

We point to God's Power *only* out of the Power to which we point. We embolden our inspirations *only* out of the Otherness in which we embolden. We see eternal visions *only* out of the Eternity in which we envision.

Further, none of the "new leader" traits benefits from our mistaken idea of "spiritual authority." No one, for example, can claim "spiritual authority" for themselves. It can never be assumed by man.

It is assigned *only* by God, and it has *only* His spiritual means at its disposal.

So future spiritual "authority" retains only its original meaning—only its original intention. Rather than an emphasis on *controlling* others, "True authority consists in *empowering* others."[8]   Our modern notions of both "talent" and "authority" reveal *errors of pride*.

Errors of Humility

But repenting leaders also err on the flip side! Amazingly, their distorted *post*modern world also promotes *errors of humility*.

With a "naive" humility, some new leaders relinquish *all* control. They become totally passive. They permit anything and everything. Strange, for the Lord of History never needs "pushovers."

Sure, the empowerment of the laity is a necessity. Yes, the servant-hood of the clergy is a must. But the new leader never sacrifices "anything in the way of conviction and firmness."[9] He protects, for example, his community's purity of vision. He reins in anyone out of line. And he even removes the "bad apples."

For example, the smiles and wiles of destructive "demons"—whether intentional or unintentional—are never allowed to take over.

In a similar naive humility, new leaders also misread the ideals of "openness," "honesty," and "authenticity." With juvenile folly, they "let it all hang out." With uncautious candor, they shamefully expose their vulnerabilities.

Then. . . . Problems far worse than shame show up:

Few "Christian" followers are mature enough to handle the intimate secrets of their leaders. Most followers easily succumb to gossip, and some even take advantage of a leader's weakness. In short, things can get "unholy" really fast.

There's a difference between "reality TV" and true transparency. There's a difference between dishonoring the work of God in our lives and walking in transfigured humility. And, there's a difference between trivializing one's anointing and walking in the grace of that anointing.

"Getting It"

We're living in a new world, but we don't know it. We've reached the "tipping point" in the emerging church, but we seem unconcerned. More than ever, we need new leaders—*spiritual* leaders. Yet, their roles are not indigenous to any idea of American, modern, postmodern, corporate, religious, or any other present notion of "leadership."

We're still confusing the "rescuers" with those needing "rescuing."

Profound change will be the price of our survival. That change will include spiritual integrity in the practice of paradox, enigma, mystery, and metaphor. That change will include prophetic boldness in the pursuit of a proactive, incarnate life. And, that change will include humble risk in the purposeful power of spiritual gifts.

As computer intelligence increases, the leading of the Holy Spirit will be the only advantage we have left. And, in that moment, the difference between the right leader and the "almost" right leader will be the difference between those who "get it" and those who "don't get it."

Endnotes

1. Matthew 20:20-28, *The Amplified Bible*.

2. A few of the many contradictions in the life of St. Paul.

3. C. S. Lewis, quoted in Leanne Payne, *Real Presence* (Grand Rapids: Baker Books, 2000) p. 143, 144.

4. In this context, the "Word made flesh" is ***anytime*** Divine inspiration takes on earthly form—as in the prophetic arts.

5. An old Portugese proverb.

6. Romans 4:17, *King James Bible*.

7. Hebrews 11:1.

8. Fritjof Capra, *The Hidden Connections*: *Integrating the Biological, Cognitive, and Social Dimensions of Life into a Science of Sustainability* (New York: Doubleday, 2002) p. 89, 100.

9. Eugene H. Peterson, *The Message//Remix: The Bible in Contemporary Language* (Colorado Springs: NavPress, 2003) p. 2162.

A NEW KINDNESS

Bigger Than Us

"'Emergent' could be very short lived.
This whole thing could blow up over
politics or theology or broken friend-
ships or whatever. I don't hold any
grand illusions over how long this
thing will be around."[1]

Emerging church leaders face the greatest promise or the greatest
peril in the history of the church. It can go either way. But why
lose for losing? Why make the world suffer for our immaturity and
excess? Yes, the Lord will win with us or without us, but why must
we become one more fatal footnote to church history.

For too long, I've talked critically and caustically about the need for
the church to renew itself. But a dear friend, near his death, told me,
"Do you want to know how to change the church? You change
yourself." That hit hard, and it still hits hard! Yet, it's true. Each of
us—with profound apology and kindness—must start all over again.

Yet tragically, our mistakes have already turned the clock back on the
emerging church. Still more disheartening, history tells us we're
running out of time. And, making matters worse, people won't listen
to us until they trust us, and trust *takes time*.

So pray that the Lord *gives us* time.

Yet, this change doesn't demand mere change. It doesn't even
demand "improvement." Our notion of "postmodern," for example,
implies an unbroken line between "before" and "after." But this
notion couldn't be further from the truth. History has broken the
line! Our old epistemology (how-we-know-what-we-know) is over.
"Before" and "after" no longer have anything in common. Once we

understand where the Lord of History is taking us, we'll call this "postmodern" moment something totally other.

We're like ants crawling on a huge wall painting. Each sees only a little piece of its time in history. And, though brief flashes of light reveal larger images, these images make no sense in the light of past understandings. In other words, something big is happening. Bigger than what we're doing. Bigger than what we're predicting.

That's the reason the "emerging church" movement is *not* about the "emerging church." Any effort to turn it into an "organization" misses the meaning of the moment. For the emerging "Body of Christ" is only a vision—only a seed—only a knowing yet unborn. Once we hammer it into ideas, doctrines, and dollars, the movement is finished. Something else will take its place.

Today's emerging church began as a "chrysalis"—the quickening *before* the "butterfly." It wasn't an organization, it was an organism—it wasn't an institution, it was a living system—it wasn't a structure, it was a spontaneous response to the hastening of history. And now, it's still too soon for its leaders to describe "what is." They must continue describing, instead, "what is coming to be."

A "cult," by the way, can be defined as "something popular or fashionable among a particular section of society." Cult or not, the in-house theologies, philosophies, and worldviews of the emerging church will not win the world. For the emerging church does not "own" the church of the future or anything else!

After all, the "Word made flesh" shows up wherever it wills. It appears in endless forms, both within and without the emerging church. If we share in this Word, then we must share in its many forms. All people, for example, encounter God, and—in one way or another—God encounters them. So elitism and arrogance among emerging church leaders are totally inappropriate.

We need those who are ***not*** us. And they need us.

The whole world yearns for kindness, and we would do well to share this common gospel. People only want to know if the messenger loves them. And they want to know if the messenger can graciously and patiently wait for stragglers to "get to the party." After that, everything else will fall into place.

This is the transcendent and transparent sharing the new church seeks. It's a church of "implicit" messages rather than "explicit" messages. It's a church of passion that expands toward something larger than us. And, it's a church with visions more real than the world in which we now live.

The Lord of History has moved beyond history. If the emerging church "gets it," the world will "get it."

Goodbye modernism. Goodbye postmodernism. Welcome Holy Spirit.

"Why can't you read the signs of the times?"[2]
Matthew 16:3

Endnotes

1. Anonymous, to protect an emerging leader.

2. Eugene H. Peterson, *The Message//Remix: The Bible in Contemporary Language* (Colorado Springs: NavPress, 2003) p. 2003.

ABOUT THE AUTHOR

Dr. Thomas Hohstadt has achieved recognition in several fields: international symphony conductor, author, lecturer, recording artist, composer, and soloist. A Fulbright scholar, he holds four advanced degrees from the Eastman School of Music and the Vienna *Akademie für Musik*. A twenty-eight-year conducting career includes positions with the Eastman School of Music; the Honolulu, Amarillo, and Midland-Odessa Symphonies; and guest appearances in eight nations.

Hohstadt has authored 6 award-winning books and 75 magazine and Web articles. His book, ***Dying To Live***, has become a classic on the future of the church. It was selected by Australia's Rowland Croucher as one of the top 100 books every thoughtful Christian should read. The Rand Corporation nominated it for one of the top "50 Books for Thinking About the Future Human Condition." And America's Bill Easum put it on his list of the "top 10 books of this decade."

Zondervan published ***Dying to Live*** in Spanish, and Abingdon released an ebook version under the title, ***A Prophetic Compass for the Emerging Church***.

Hohstadt is a well-known, online adviser to church leaders throughout the world. Christians in one hundred and twenty nations follow his **FutureChurch.net**. Widely quoted and published on the Internet, over thirteen hundred sites link to FutureChurch. Recently, he participated in a summit of the top 30 thinkers from 3 continents on "The Apostolic Mission in the Emerging World."

Breaking barriers in many fields, Tom enjoys unusually wide

influence—from conservative to liberal and from Pentecostal to intellectual. Recognized especially in the arts, his "What Makes Music Christian?" finds repeated publication on the web. And his clarity on Hebrew *damah* provided the artistic breakthrough for the Damah Film Festival.

Hohstadt's work has been called "a prophet's vision wedded to a scholar's learning."